FROZEN in TIME

FROZEN IN TIME

CLARENCE BIRDSEYE'S OUTRAGEOUS IDEA ABOUT FROZEN FOOD

MARK KURLANSKY

DELACORTE PRESS

Visit us on the Web! randomhousekids.com

Educators and librarians, for a variety of teaching tools, visit us at
RHTeachersLibrarians.com

Library of Congress Cataloging-in-Publication Data
Kurlansky, Mark.
Frozen in time : Clarence Birdseye's outrageous idea about frozen food /
Mark Kurlansky.
pages cm
Audience: Age 10 and up.
ISBN 978-0-385-74388-4 (hardback) —
ISBN 978-0-375-99135-6 (library binding) —
ISBN 978-0-385-37243-5 (ebook) — ISBN 978-0-385-37244-2 (pbk.)
1. Birdseye, Clarence, 1886–1956—Juvenile literature. 2. Frozen foods
industry—United States—History—Juvenile literature. 3. Inventors—United
States—Biography—Juvenile literature. 4. Businessmen—United States—
Biography—Juvenile literature. I. Title.
HD9217.U52B5753 2014
338.7'664—dc23
[B]
2014017840

The text of this book is set in 11.75-point Goudy Old Style.
Book design by Trish Parcell

Printed in the United States of America
10 9 8 7 6 5 4 3 2 1
First Edition

To the memory of the too-short but good life of

Cooper Dean Stock,

a boy of curiosity and laughter

contents

PROLOGUE

The Nerds of the Industrial Revolution

It's easy to take for granted the food we eat today. When you open the freezer to take out a pizza or a bag of peas or a box of waffles, you're probably not thinking about who "invented" frozen food. But someone did, and that man was Clarence Birdseye. Some people might say that this is a book about a nerd, but it is really a book about a man who started a food revolution.

Clarence Birdseye was one of those kids who don't quite fit in. He was intensely interested in things his peers were not thinking much about. He did not care about what was hip or fashionable, and he was sometimes ridiculed for his peculiar interests. He didn't have enough money to finish college and was forced to drop out, yet he ultimately made a fortune off one of his ideas.

Although this story isn't from the headlines of today, it might sound like it's happening now. A list of people who changed the world in our time would include Bill Gates, a man who got his start devising a computer program for tic-tac-toe in the eighth grade; spent most of high school and college creating other programs; dropped out of Harvard to start his own software company, Microsoft, at age twenty; and soon became the wealthiest man in the world. And Mark Zuckerberg, who started Facebook with a group of college friends. Like Gates, Zuckerberg didn't finish college and started his own business, which made him a billionaire by age twenty-three.

Twenty-first-century inventors achieve fame and fortune at a much earlier age than their nineteenth- and twentieth-century counterparts. In truth, there have always been life-changing inventions, and the inventors from a century ago were just like the young people of today. They were people who looked at what could be created and found innovative ways to make new projects happen.

When Clarence Birdseye was alive, from the late nineteenth to the mid-twentieth century, the rate at which original, life-changing inventions were being developed and sold was dazzling. These dramatic inventions included electric lights, automobiles, the phonograph, and even the airplane, as well as smaller ideas, such as portable cameras, drinking straws, Styrofoam, fountain pens, and barbed wire.

Birdseye's interest in industrial food is not surprising, as there were many before him who made their fortunes from products like flavored gelatin, dried cereal, processed cheese, or sliced bread. Making a fortune on developing a really melty fake cheese is no stranger than selling an app that takes photos of your dog in a hat for more than a billion dollars. The key to invention is simply imagining something.

CHAPTER ONE

A Fast-Changing World

If Clarence Birdseye hadn't been born in Brooklyn (which was not part of New York City in the 1880s) on December 9, 1886, his life might have been very different. Brooklyn was the third-largest city in the United States and one of the fastest growing. Between 1880 and 1890, the population of Brooklyn increased by more than a third, to 806,343. One of the factors that made such growth possible was refrigeration. When populations of a few hundred thousand people or more lived in a concentrated area that produced no food, it was difficult to supply and distribute the needed quantities of fresh and nutritious food every day. Once people were able to buy a few days' worth of groceries and refrigerate them, population density began to rise.

A critical component of refrigeration around the world was ice generated in winter on the frozen lakes of upstate New York and New England and stored year-round in ice-houses along the Hudson River. There the ice was kept insulated with sawdust until it could be shipped to cities. The storehouses supplied New York City with more than one million tons of ice every year for food and drinks.

The pleasure of enjoying iced drinks on a hot day had been a luxury for the wealthy since Roman times, but in New York City in the late nineteenth century, it became commonplace. Almost half of Manhattanites and Brooklynites stored food in their homes inside insulated boxes chilled by blocks of ice. A few people even had artificially chilled refrigerators, though at that time they were dangerous and clumsy electric machines with unpredictable motors and leaky fluids.

Birdseye was born into this world of iced drinks and refrigeration. He and other New Yorkers lived in a city where ice was used more than anywhere else in the world.

Even though Birdseye lived most of his life in the twentieth century, he spent his formative years in the late 1800s and grew up to become a nineteenth-century man. He was born at the height of the Industrial Revolution, and though he worked in an age of electronic invention, all his inventions would be mechanical, never electronic.

When Birdseye was born, the popular heroes were the inventors of the Industrial Revolution, who created that great shift from products made by hand in workshops to products made by machines in factories. He grew up in a time when industry was admired and industrializing was considered an admirable feat, as creating new technological gadgets is today.

In Birdseye's age the world was rapidly becoming industrialized, yet the food industry lagged behind and was still mostly artisanal. Not everyone had an icebox, and the preservation of refrigerated food had not been perfected. People had to rely almost exclusively on fresh produce.

Yet the world had evolved, thanks to new inventions. In 1876, just ten years before Birdseye was born, Alexander Graham Bell invented the telephone. The following year Thomas Edison invented the phonograph. In 1878 Joseph Wilson Swan, a British inventor, patented the first incandescent lightbulb and lit his home with electric lights. The year before Birdseye was born, a German engineer named Karl Benz—perhaps as important in his day as Bill Gates is today—patented the first automobile for practical use: a three-wheeled vehicle powered by an internal combustion engine, the kind still used in cars today, which is fueled by periodically filling the tank with gasoline. Also in 1885, another German, Gottlieb Daimler, built the first gas-powered motorcycle; the following year he built the first four-wheeled automobile.

Among the other important inventors at the time of Birdseye's birth was George Eastman, who was to have a profound effect on Birdseye. In 1884 Eastman patented roll film, and in 1888 he produced a lightweight camera that used the film, naming it the Kodak camera. His company, the Eastman Kodak Company, was the first major supplier of photographic equipment and gave birth to amateur photography, a passionate hobby of the young Clarence Birdseye. These cameras were to him and his generation what the latest cell phones and tablets are to us today.

In 1884 the synthetic-cloth industry began when a French chemist, Louis-Marie-Hilaire Bernigaud, Comte de

Chardonnet, patented a process to make artificial silk, which a decade later became known as rayon. That same year Lewis Waterman, a Brooklyn insurance agent, frustrated with the inefficient pens of the day, invented the capillary-feeding fountain pen, the first practical alternative to a pen dipped in an inkwell. Also in 1879 James Ritty, an Ohio barkeeper, became the first manufacturer of cash registers, which he had invented. In 1885, the American inventor Hiram Maxim demonstrated the first machine gun to the British army. In 1886, Birdseye's birth year, in addition to Daimler's automobile, Coca-Cola and the first washing machine were invented. The following year barbed wire, which divided up the open range and changed the character of the American West, as well as contact lenses, were patented. In 1888 Marvin Stone, an Ohio-born inventor, came out with the first paper drinking straw. In 1892 Joshua Pusey, a cigar-smoking attorney from Pennsylvania, invented the matchbook. In 1891, when Birdseye was four years old, Jesse Reno invented the escalator. Typical for his generation, Reno was part inventor and part entrepreneur, creating a sensation in Birdseye's native Brooklyn when he showcased the escalator for two weeks as a ride at the Coney Island amusement park. It was then featured on the Manhattan side of the Brooklyn Bridge—itself still a sensation as the longest suspension bridge in the world, connecting Brooklyn and Manhattan for the first time in 1883.

EUROPEAN INVENTIONS

Birdseye grew up in a time when new devices seemed to be coming out every week, garnering a great deal of public attention with claims that they would change everyone's life. Young people in particular embraced the new devices. It was an exciting time to be growing up.

In the nineteenth century there was a notable difference between the culture of American inventors and that of European inventors. In America, when someone came up with a new industrial idea, he registered it with the government, which gave the inventor a patent to establish his authorship of the idea. Americans had a Puritanical belief that anyone who invented something had a moral obligation to put it to useful service, so they thought inventions were of little value without practical and commercial applications. While Europe had the same patent-registry procedure, European inventors worked on patents that were merely theoretical, lest they give the impression of harboring lowbrow commercial interests. They did not have a capitalist view; they did not want to use inventions to make money.

There were, of course, exceptions on both sides. One was Dr. John Gorrie, who ran a hospital for the US Navy in Apalachicola, Florida, that treated victims of yellow fever and malaria. He invented a primitive form of air conditioning in the 1840s that produced artificial ice by expanding compressed air. Gorrie cooled his hospital and his home with his device but was so attacked by religious conservatives for interfering with God's design that he published his ideas in the *Commercial Advertiser* under a pseudonym. Not realizing who the writer was, the editor of the publication criticized the author for failing to put his ideas into service. It would be sixty years before modern air conditioning was developed, at the beginning of the twentieth century.

Then there was Robert Fulton, the father of the steamboat, an American inventor who actually benefited from the European view. The steamboat had had a long development that had nothing to do with him. It was a European idea, as was the steam engine. A Frenchman, Denis Papin, invented a piston steam engine in 1690 and a man-powered paddlewheel steamboat in 1704 but failed to attract any interest in them. The Scottish engineer James Watt built a greatly improved steam engine at the time of the American Revolution. But although the French, the Germans, the British, and the Americans built various steam-powered vessels, there were no *commercially* successful steamboats until Fulton's. So the great inventor Robert Fulton did not exactly invent anything. Rather, he put the right kind of engine in the right kind of vessel and established a commercial run on the right route. Earlier lines existed, but they were established on less profitable routes or on routes that already had good land transportation.

Fulton established his line in 1807 on the East River in Manhattan, making trips up the Hudson to Albany, the state capital. It was successful, in part because there was no good land route for hauling freight between these two important centers. Fulton is today often erroneously remembered as the inventor of the steamboat—in much the same way that Birdseye is erroneously remembered as the inventor of fast freezing. The real reason we still know the name Fulton is that he launched an industry by showing that money could be made from steamboats and that it was a commercially important idea.

Birdseye grew up in a world where mere concepts and

ideas were not enough. Inventors were expected to solve a problem, form a company, and, hopefully, earn a fortune. Alexander Graham Bell, a Scot who moved to Canada and then to America, was fairly well known, not only as the inventor of the telephone but also as the founder of the first telephone company, the Bell Telephone Company, in 1877. By the time Birdseye was born, just nine years later, Bell Telephone had placed phones in 150,000 homes and offices.

In 1876 Thomas Edison came to the public's attention for selling his telegraph idea to Western Union for a surprising $10,000. Then in 1880 he created another industry, Edison Lampworks, which manufactured 50,000 lightbulbs annually. When Edison developed an idea, which he did with astounding regularity, he built a company. This was the model Birdseye and his American contemporaries would follow.

CHAPTER TWO

Bugs Begins

Clarence Birdseye understood that he had a funny name, so he quickly dropped the Clarence and went by Bob for the rest of his life. Even people today who know the frozen-food brand Birds Eye, with its descending bird as a symbol, are often surprised that there actually *was* someone with such an odd name. All his life people had trouble believing that Birdseye was really his name. One of his favorite stories was how he once found himself in San Francisco, short on money, and wanted to cash a check. He called the local branch of General Foods' Birds Eye Division, a company named after him, explained his problem, and gave his name. The man on the other end of the line told him if he stopped kidding and gave his real name, he would connect him with someone.

Birdseye, who loved to tell stories, had another favorite, about the origin of his name. According to him, it was originally two words—Bird's Eye. In his story the young page to an English queen saw a large hawk swoop down toward her majesty. "This page boy ancestor of mine, according to the records, took out his trusty bow and arrow and shot that bird right in the eye," Birdseye would explain. "The queen was so tickled, she gave him the name right on the spot." He never produced these records, so there is reason for suspicion.

However, Birdseye loved hunting and hyperbolic tales of improbable shots. A great influence of the nineteenth century that would never leave him was the romance of the American West, which combined those two loves. He was born in a time when people who did not adjust well to life on the East Coast often went west, hoping for better, only to live with great deprivation and often violence. There was a brutal war of extermination against the native tribes throughout the territories. In 1886, Birdseye's birth year, the US Army, having failed to capture Chiricahua Apache leader Geronimo in Arizona, negotiated a treaty with him, which was never honored. The last action of the US Army against the native tribes took place when Birdseye was four years old. It was the shooting of three hundred mostly unarmed Lakota Sioux men, women, and children at their Pine Ridge, South Dakota, reservation by the Wounded Knee Creek on December 29, 1890.

Once the bloodshed ended, the western romance began, both on the East Coast and in Europe. Western landscapes became popular, as did rugs and other Indian artifacts. Romantic novels of western adventure were widely read; lacking massacres and broken treaties, the battles were represented as gripping but fair fights. Birdseye loved these spirited tales as a boy, and in fact all his life, and cowboys, hunters, and trappers fascinated him. His favorite writer was George Alfred Henty, a nineteenth-century English war correspondent turned popular novelist who wrote adventure stories, usually for boys. The lead characters were always highly intelligent, extremely resourceful, and courageous. He wrote 122 novels before he died, in 1902. Birdseye's favorite Henty novel was his 1891 *Redskin and Cowboy*. It is the tale of an English boy who is forced to leave the safety and quiet of his uncle's home and journey to the American West, where he meets such characters as Straight Charley, Bronco Harry, and Lightning Hugh. Although most Henty novels are thought of as children's books, Birdseye read them and other westerns his entire life, rereading his favorites.

As a kid growing up in Brooklyn, Birdseye dreamed of being a smart, capable young hero of a Henty novel. During his childhood, in the 1880s and '90s, several historians named Buffalo Bill Cody the most famous person in the world. He had earned his nickname after having been hired by the Kansas Pacific Railroad to keep the rail workers supplied with buffalo meat. According to legend, in eight months between 1867 and 1868 he killed 4,280 buffalo (actually bison). This kind of killing was another nineteenth-century American reality that strongly influenced Birdseye.

Historians have labeled the second half of the nineteenth century the age of extermination. The American bison herd, the largest land animal herd ever recorded, was by the late nineteenth century reduced from the tens of millions that once roamed the plains to only a few hundred. Today about 200,000 live on preserves and ranches. Passenger pigeons, which were thought to number five billion when Europeans started coming to North America and may have represented as much as 40 percent of the continent's bird population, were killed for cheap food. The last passenger pigeon passed away in a Cincinnati zoo in the early twentieth century.

In the nineteenth century four hundred thousand skunks, five hundred thousand raccoons, and two million muskrats were killed in a typical year. Beaver, seal, and sea otters were all victims. Gradually, led by such writers as Ralph Waldo Emerson, Henry David Thoreau, and John Muir, Americans started to grow concerned about the slaughter, and the government began regulating hunting. At several points in his youth Birdseye came into conflict with the new regulations.

Bob Birdseye wanted to be a colorful character, and in 1951 he wrote, "The public customarily thinks of me as an inventor . . . but inventing is only one of my lines. I am also a bank director, a president of companies, a fisherman, an author, an engineer, a cook, a naturalist, a stockholder, a consultant, and a dock-walloper." Clarence Frank Birdseye, Bob's father, for whom he was named, did not pursue a life of adventure. Born in 1854, he attended an elite Brooklyn school, graduated from Amherst College in 1874 and Columbia Law School in 1877, and, like his father and grandfather, became a prominent attorney. He wrote numerous books, often on education, such as *The Reorganization of Our Colleges* and *Individual Training in Our Colleges*, as well as a number of legal textbooks, including his 1879 revision of New York State code and statutory law, which became a standard legal textbook.

Clarence Senior married Ada Jane Underwood, Bob's mother, who was born in Brooklyn a year after he was, in 1855. If the urge toward industrial invention has a genetic strain, Bob did not inherit it from the legalistic Birdseyes but from his mother's side. Ada's father, Henry Underwood, was a belt manufacturer. The machines of the Industrial Revolution ran on belts that connected motors to working parts through pulleys. Henry Underwood reasoned that the belts would stop slipping if they had more surfaces on the pulleys. So rather than a flat or rounded belt, he built a trapezoidal one to run through pulleys with angular grooves. His invention did not have the impact of electric lightbulbs, or even frozen food, but it improved many machines, and when Underwood patented his idea, it merited mention in the April 1860 edition of *Scientific American* in their roundup of new inventions. Ada's father was the first American manufacturer of leather belts, which he later improved, creating cotton-leather belts in the 1890s. Underwood's belts, and those inspired by his inventions, were critical to the growth of industrial machine technology and were a small but essential part of the development of refrigeration machines.

Clarence and Ada had nine children, but one of the twin girls born two years before Bob died before she was a year old. Bob was their sixth child. There is not a great deal known about Bob's relationship with his seven siblings. His older brothers Kellogg and Henry became businessmen, to whom he often turned for advice, and he seemed particularly fond of his brother Roger Williams Birdseye, born four years after him. In Bob's letters and journals his siblings are only occasionally mentioned, but he did name his two sons after Kellogg and Henry. The Birdseyes were a large family in which relatives were available for advice and connections. In the forty years when young, restless Bob was rummaging through opportunities looking for his career, relatives constantly aided him.

Young Bob showed few signs—or at least few were recorded—of being the garrulous social person he became as an adult. He disliked organized sports and other activities most boys were expected to participate in. It is not known if he had close friends. Most descriptions of the boy have him alone in nature. At an early age he had decided that what was important in life was to find his own way.

When he was about eight years old, the family bought a farm in Orient, New York, at the end of the North Fork of Long Island. The farm was named Wyndiecote, and Bob so loved it that he would use the name repeatedly for his homes as an adult, since he viewed it as his ideal home. He claimed to like "nothing better . . . than to tramp alone through fields or along the seashore studying the birds and other wildlife which I encountered." It was his mother, Ada, who first noticed that the boy was at heart a naturalist, which is defined as a keen observer of nature.

When Bob was ten years old, he became fixated, in that way ten-year-olds do, on something he had to have. In his case he just had to have a shotgun, which his parents weren't willing to buy for him. In his young mind hunting was not only an essential part of enjoying nature but also a way of profiting from the natural resources available to him. In his walks through the marshes around the sprawling Birdseye farm, he had noticed a great number of muskrats—large, homely, awkward, two-foot-long bundles of fur. Bob wondered where there would be a market for these large rodents. He wrote to Dr. William T. Hornaday, the director of the Bronx Zoo, and asked him if he would be interested in acquiring some muskrats. Hornaday wrote back, explaining that he already had all the muskrats he could use, but he referred him to an English aristocrat who was stocking an estate. The ten-year-old went into the marshes and set traps until he had twelve live muskrats, which he shipped to England. Nine of the muskrats survived the trip, and the Englishman paid him $1 for each. With that $9 Bob bought a single-barrel shotgun. Making a profit from ideas was always a fundamental belief of Birdseye's.

The following year, in the winter of 1897, after learning how to preserve and stuff animals by reading books and asking questions at taxidermy shops, Bob placed an ad in a sports magazine for "the American School of Taxidermy," offering courses at modest rates. It is easy to imagine the comical scene ensuing when someone wishing to learn more from the ad discovered that not only the professor but the entire school consisted of an eleven-year-old boy. Unfortunately there is no record of anyone responding to the advertisement.

When Bob was entering high school, the family moved to Montclair, New Jersey. Life in the new suburban town was still not one of adventure. In high school, although his interests lay primarily in science, he also took a cooking class. At the time progressive women wanted to help the female population have careers outside the home, so there was an increase in the number of cooking classes, which taught women to prepare food quickly so they would have time to keep a job but still have dinner on the table when their husbands returned home. Such classes grew out of a mid-nineteenth-century movement to educate women on home management. (Men were not taught to be concerned with such matters.) Eventually those classes would be called home economics and would cover the process of cooking and the science of nutrition.

By the time Birdseye was in high school, frugal, scientific, pragmatic, nutritious cooking was the established approach. His older sister Miriam, who graduated from Smith College in 1901 and earned a graduate degree in domestic science from Pratt Institute in 1907, may also have influenced Bob. She started as a home economics teacher in New York City and later became a prominent nutritionist. Another sister, Katherine, two years older than Bob and the surviving twin, would later marry one John Lang, divorce him, settle in Atlantic City, New Jersey, and become president and general manager of Mrs. Lang's Candy Kitchen, which sold candy in stores along the boardwalk. Little is known about life in the Ada and Clarence Senior household that would have led two of their children toward distinguished careers in food and a third to open a specialty food store.

The summer after high school Bob moved to New York City but did not find a lot of opportunities for a young man seeking an original life. He worked first as an inspector for the city sanitation department and then as a $3-a-week office boy in a Wall Street financial firm. In the fall his parents sent him off to Amherst College, in Massachusetts.

Amherst was the Birdseye family school. But Bob's interests were different from those of his father and brothers.

Amherst was a liberal arts college with no emphasis on science, Bob's major. Science majors were awarded bachelor of arts degrees, like literature majors. There was no bachelor of science degree.

In his first year Bob was an honors student in science but only average in everything else, including physical education. He did particularly badly in Spanish, a language for which he saw no use until much later in his life. However, Birdseye studied under respected professors of the day. His professor of biology, his favorite subject, was John Mason Tyler, who had graduated from Amherst in 1873, when the writings of Charles Darwin that were to be the foundation of modern biology were fresh off the press and not yet part of the accepted teachings in the field. Benjamin Kendall Emerson, with whom Bob hoped to study geology, graduated from Amherst in 1865, the year the Civil War ended. Edward Hitchcock, a doctor who taught physiology and anatomy and was a pioneer in the physical education program with which Bob struggled, was born in the town of Amherst in 1828, the year construction began on the first passenger railroad in the United States and Noah Webster's dictionary of the American language was published.

There was not much opportunity for western-style adventure at Amherst. Birdseye wrote in later life that he used to spend free time at Amherst wandering the fields with his shotgun on his shoulder. His fellow classmates called him Bugs because he was forever examining some bug or rodent in the countryside.

While out on one of his walks, Birdseye "suddenly . . .

came upon an open spring-hole where thousands of small frogs were congregating—layers and layers of them came to hibernate for the winter. 'What are those frogs good for?' I asked myself." And though seven years had passed, Birdseye thought he would try the Bronx Zoo again, since they had previously helped him sell the muskrats. He knew that the zoo had frog-eating reptiles that needed to be fed, and they said yes, they did want the frogs. They asked that he ship them alive, since reptiles eat only live prey, so Birdseye wrapped them in wet burlap and sent them to the zoo. For this he earned $115, which was more than the $110 annual tuition at Amherst.

On another occasion Birdseye wandered behind the town butcher shop and discovered an infestation of rodents. What would have been just a horrible black rat to most people, Bob recognized as a nearly extinct species, and he found a geneticist at Columbia University who was willing to pay $135 for a shipment of them.

He avoided talking about catching the frogs and rats and other such activities because they led to mockery, and he felt isolated at Amherst. He did not like being called Bugs, but for Bob happiness always came from answering his own calling, being who he was. Writing about his college days later, Bob said, "I did not realize at the time, as I have discovered since, that anyone who attempts anything original in this world must expect a bit of ridicule." In fact, he would come to understand that accepting ridicule was one of the keys to success.

• • •

After spending the summer between his freshman and sophomore years going west at last, to the New Mexico Territory, to work with the US Biological Survey, Birdseye returned to Amherst in the fall. He seemed to find his rhythm in school that year. Although he played no sports, he learned to do well in gym. He also joined a fraternity. (His father was a great believer in fraternities and had even written a book on the subject.) By spring 1908 young Bugs scored 96 percent in biology and had almost a 90 average. In those less competitive days, it was perfectly acceptable to be a C student; an A student was an unusual phenomenon. Bob was well on his way to being a brilliant student. He applied to take special advanced biology and geology classes.

But that year, for reasons that are not clear, the Birdseyes suffered a financial crisis, and there was no more money for schooling. On December 31, 1908, Bob wrote the school registrar, "It will almost certainly be necessary for me to go through the rest of this year without any financial aid from home; and to this I must borrow about $300—$150 or $200 at once. Is there a student loan fund at Amherst and if there is can I secure the necessary money at not more than six percent interest and for one or two years."

Apparently, he was not given a loan, because after spring 1909 he dropped out of college. This was the end of his formal education.

What was he to do with only two years of college? Without a college degree, he could not become the fourth generation of distinguished Birdseye attorneys, but he was not likely to have done that anyway. He had wanted to go to school to learn, not to launch a career. He could have returned to Wall

Street and tried to make his mark in business. New York was full of possibilities. But that was not what Birdseye was inclined to do. When he was in his sixties, he said, "Any youth who makes security his goal shackles himself at the very start of life's race." Birdseye was not looking for financial security. He was looking for adventure. And where did you find adventure in 1909? Out west.

CHAPTER THREE

Bob Goes West

After Bob left college, he resumed his job from the previous summer with the US Biological Survey in the New Mexico and Arizona territories. Both territories were still considered a part of the western frontier, even though in 1901 a railroad line extended to the Grand Canyon and a tourist village was built there, stimulating the birth of southwestern tourism. With the primary mode of transportation still horses and the territories lacking the necessary infrastructure to apply for statehood, it wasn't until 1912 that New Mexico and Arizona would become the forty-seventh and forty-eighth states.

The primary function of the US Biological Survey—a branch of the Department of Agriculture—was to ask farmers and ranchers which animals bothered them and then to set up campaigns to eradicate those species. At the top of the list were wolves and coyotes, predators hated by ranchers because they ate livestock. The survey hired hunters and trappers to get rid of them. In 1907 alone the program killed

544 coyotes in New Mexico and 1,424 more in Arizona. There was considerable controversy about the vicious steel traps that would hold an animal by the leg until it starved to death. In the 1920s the survey began poisoning the animals with carcasses injected with strychnine, producing a slow and agonizing but certain death. Contemporary attitudes regarding the treatment of wildlife have changed and practices deemed cruel have been banned, but in Birdseye's time the big predators—wolves, coyotes, bobcats, and mountain lions—were hunted or trapped.

According to Birdseye, the US Biological Survey originally hired him as an "assistant naturalist . . . [part of a] scientific party, which was studying birds and mammals in New Mexico and Arizona." At the time the survey sent naturalists throughout the territories by horseback estimating animal populations and studying their habits, especially what the large predators preyed on. The survey largely discredited ranchers' claim that the wild predators were destroying livestock: while this did happen, livestock were not the primary or preferred prey of any of these animals. In the case of coyotes, the survey found that they largely ate mice, yet this did not stop the campaign against them.

Wandering the western frontier on horseback with a rifle, shooting wildlife, Bob was living a childhood dream. Again he thought of a business opportunity. Bob knew that Indian trading posts offered only 25 cents for a coyote or bobcat fur, but he felt sure that they were worth more than that. When he returned to New York at the end of the summer, finding first a job with an insurance company and later one with the city's Department of Sanitation as a "snow checker"—the man who maintains records on the amount of snow removed from city streets after a blizzard—he discovered that furriers in New York would pay $1.25 each for bobcat and coyote pelts. Bob wrote to the traders to whom he had spoken in the Southwest and offered them 50 cents for pelts, double the trading posts' rate, and sold the pelts in New York himself for a 75-cent profit. He earned $600 on his fur trading that winter and decided to return to the Southwest the next summer.

Living in the Southwest, Bob acquired some exotic food habits that remained with him all his life. When he found something in nature, Birdseye always wondered what it would taste like and what would be the best way to cook it. He liked his rattlesnake cut in slices, dusted with flour, and then fried in salt pork. While camped on one of the then-undeveloped rims of the Grand Canyon, the naturalists discovered that their only provision, pork belly, had gone rancid. Bob Birdseye wasn't worried and went off to find dinner. He gathered field mice, chipmunks, gophers, and even a few pack rats, which he carefully skinned and gutted before wrapping them all in cheesecloth. Finally he simmered the meat in a pot of boiling water. He praised the resulting stew, though there is no record of anyone else sharing his enthusiasm.

Birdseye's colleagues rarely partook of his specialties, preferring canned food—typically beans, corn, and tomatoes—carried by packhorse as they traveled the countryside. Bob was struck by the extent to which westerners lived on food from a can and noticed that there seemed to be a great need for preserved food. As he traveled by horse, he would often see something sparkling in the sun on the horizon, only to realize that he was approaching a ranch or a town, both of which were always marked by piles of discarded cans. He regarded canning as an inferior way of preserving food, because the food had to be reheated and was no longer in its fresh state. Even so, he had a great fondness for it. "He just loved canned food," said Gypsy, the wife of his oldest son, Kellogg. It reminded Birdseye of his youth, when he rode in the West, though he played a major role in the decline of canned food in the American diet.

As winter approached in 1910, Birdseye decided to go to Washington, D.C., to work for the Department of Agriculture. At the time, the capital was a genteel Southern town of 331,000 people with horse-drawn carriages and hitching posts, but it was growing fast in both population and building construction. Washington could have become a high-rise megalopolis like Manhattan, but in that year a law was passed restricting building heights to the width of the adjacent street plus twenty feet, so they have remained the same as they were when Bob moved there.

While in Washington, Bob met the adventurous men of the National Geographic Society, including C. Hart Merriam, one of its thirty-three founding members and the head of the US Biological Survey. When the society was formed, in 1888, it was led by Gardiner Hubbard, a Boston lawyer who had financed Alexander Graham Bell's development of the telephone and had been the first president of the Bell Telephone Company. He declared, "The more we know, the greater we find is our ignorance. Because we know so little, we have formed this society for the increase and diffusion of Geographic knowledge."

This was Birdseye's kind of language, and the society's magazine spoke to that, too. At the time, there was nothing more exciting to Bob and other adventurous young men of his generation than *National Geographic* magazine. By 1910 it had distinguished itself for exploration, investigating new ideas, and photography—all passions of young Birdseye. Part of what made the magazine exciting was the use of new photographic technology. To people who grew up in the late nineteenth and early twentieth centuries, portable cameras with film that had to be developed generated the excitement. *National Geographic* was said to publish the best photography of the day. In 1907 it had created a sensation with Edward S. Curtis's portraits of American Indians. Bob, like many others of his generation, was enthralled with the possibilities of photography, and among his dreams he envisioned becoming a photographer, traveling to exotic places to record the landscape and customs.

Henry Gannett, another of the society's thirty-three founders, was chief geographer for the US Geological Survey, an organization whose topographical maps of the American West in the late nineteenth century set a new standard for mapmaking. Henry's younger cousin Samuel was also among the founders, and was a geographer with the US Geological Survey. As a surveyor, he defined the borders of several new western states. The West still had uncharted territory. To young people like Bob who longed to wander the American West, the maps were treasures.

Bob was meeting men who to him were legends, and he found their tales of exploration spellbinding. One of the most exciting adventures at the time was the exploration of the frozen lands of the north. When Bob arrived in Washington in 1909, Admiral Robert E. Peary, whom Birdseye admired, had announced that he was the first to reach the North Pole. Members of Peary's expedition had shot color photos, with a process invented in 1907, which the magazine published, along with an article detailing his trip.

Prior to his 1909 expedition, Peary was already a famous explorer, having led expeditions in Greenland and the Arctic. He traveled by dogsled and was famously photographed wearing Arctic furs, as he was known for learning Inuit ways of dress and survival. His wife sometimes accompanied him on his remarkable trips.

While reading about Peary's life was exciting, Birdseye became even more intrigued with the people living in Washington—especially Samuel Gannett's daughter, Eleanor. When they met, she was finishing her degree at George Washington University. She was a well-educated woman for her generation, as were Bob's sisters. Bob and Eleanor dated for five years, though for most of that time they didn't see each other, because he was constantly off on his adventures.

He didn't talk about being an inventor with Eleanor; even after he became one, he seldom used the word to describe himself. She could see that he had an insatiable curiosity and a great sense of adventure. Despite her quiet ways, Bob could see that Eleanor did not come from the kind of conventional home he'd had and was not looking for the kind of man who would become a prominent lawyer or work on Wall Street.

So she was not perturbed when he left on an adventure

CHAPTER FOUR

Real Bugs

In the early twentieth century, a man like Clarence Birdseye, with a love of science and adventure, would inevitably stumble into one of the great medical expeditions. Bob had been born into an exciting age of medical pioneers whose defeat of dreaded diseases made them into larger-than-life heroes. Some researchers in fact died from exposure to the illnesses they were trying to conquer.

In 1910 the US government decided to send a team of medical crusaders to the Bitterroot Mountains of Montana to combat a deadly strain of what became known as Rocky Mountain spotted fever. Few would be willing to accept the hardship, risk, and uncertainty of this project. According to legend, when the US Biological Survey was asked for volunteers, the response was "Why not ask Birdseye?" Bob was one of only two volunteers from the survey, drawn to this project by the same traits that would eventually earn him fame and fortune: boundless curiosity, fascination with the latest scientific ideas, and a thirst for adventure.

Rocky Mountain spotted fever is a life-threatening disease. Much is still unknown about how it spreads and how it acts on the human body. But in 1910 even less was understood about it. It was a uniquely American disease, occurring only in the Western Hemisphere. Its name comes from the place where it was first identified; elsewhere it had other labels, such as São Paulo fever, New World spotted fever, and American spotted fever.

There are tremendous differences in the number of people who die from the disease in different areas: in one it may kill 5 percent of victims; in another 70 percent. The reason for this remains a mystery. In 1910 the mortality rate was typically high enough that an outbreak would terrify an entire population.

A victim can have the disease for as long as two weeks without exhibiting any symptoms. Eventually he gets a sickish feeling for a few days that suggests an oncoming cold or flu. Then he may be afflicted with an extremely severe headache and painful joints, light begins to hurt his eyes, his neck becomes stiff, and he develops a dangerously high fever. At that point doctors sometimes suspect meningitis. The patient cannot sleep and at times becomes delirious. After several days of those symptoms, slightly raised red spots appear on the skin that are easily confused with measles. (Recent science has revealed that the disease organisms in the cells lining the capillaries swell and break, and blood seeps through the capillary walls.) Those tiny welts show up on the entire body, including the hands and feet. Without any treatment, many people will recover in a matter of weeks, but a significant number, especially over the age of forty, will die.

In the nineteenth century the disease was not fully understood. Records exist of an outbreak of the fever, then called black measles, in Idaho in 1896, and there are accounts of diseases with similar names among westward-moving pioneers. But until the US government began researching the outbreak in the Bitterroot Valley of western Montana in 1910, there had been no scientific study of the disease soon to be known as Rocky Mountain spotted fever.

Pathology—the study of the causes of diseases and how they spread—did not exist until Birdseye's time. Little was understood about diseases.

The exciting new age of medicine that was part of Bob Birdseye's time, an age when diseases could be identified and then conquered, began with Louis Pasteur. The French chemist demonstrated in the 1850s that fermentation was caused by the growth of organisms that were so small, they could be seen only with a microscope, and he proposed that microorganisms caused diseases.

Medical researchers armed with new knowledge and equipment began traveling the globe and conquering epidemics. Cholera was often eradicated, notably in New York City, by purifying drinking water. Bacteria were identified in outbreaks of numerous diseases, including bubonic plague, typhoid, leprosy, and tuberculosis. During the 1898 Spanish-American War, as yellow fever was decimating US troops, army physician Walter Reed went to Cuba and found that a microorganism carried by a specific species of mosquito caused yellow fever; eventually this discovery led to sanitation programs in Cuba and Panama, also hard-hit, that wiped out the disease in those areas. In 1906 construction of the Panama Canal—which shortened shipping routes between the Atlantic and the Pacific and was funded by huge investments from powerful nations, especially the United States—had been stopped by outbreaks of yellow fever among workers. Because of Reed's research, the project was able to be completed.

Montana's Bitterroot Valley was one hundred miles of wooded flatland that was previously a lakebed between the Bitterroot Mountains and the Sapphire range. The Bitterroot River runs through it, making the valley an agreeable setting sheltered by the mountain ranges. The native people were healthy, and the whites who started settling there in the mid-nineteenth century had no particular health problems until 1873, when spotted fever struck. The first documented case involved one of the few white men living in the valley, and he died from it. Later the widespread occurrence of a strange disease coincided with the spectacular expansion of the lumber industry; the west bank of the river, where the lumbering was prominent, was also where the disease was affecting people.

The advance of medicine at the turn of the century included a growth in public health institutions, and in 1901 Montana established a state board of health. A Ravalli County board of health had existed since 1896. Once there were agencies to monitor disease, they started noticing a large number of patients in the Bitterroot Valley with diagnoses such as black typhus fever, blue disease, and black fever. The spotted fever was not unique to the valley; outbreaks were also discovered in neighboring Idaho, in Colorado, Oregon, Wyoming, and possibly even earlier in California, Washington, Nevada, and Utah. However, it was a much more life-threatening disease in the Bitterroot than anywhere else. In Colorado the disease had a mortality rate of 23 percent, but in the spring of 1901 Montana had fourteen cases and all but four died, resulting in a mortality rate of 71 percent.

In Bitterroot the leading theory was that melting snow somehow caused the black measles. Though it may sound silly today, the fact was that every year there was an outbreak of the illness in the spring, just as the snow started melting, and there had been notable research suggesting that many epidemics, such as typhoid and cholera, were spread in water. In 1889 a particularly well-educated Montana physician who had studied the work on yellow fever noticed a tick on a patient and suggested that this might be significant.

SCIENCE

In 1902 a new crop of investigators arrived in the Bitterroot Valley in the spring, as the disease never struck before mid-March. Two of the scientists were pathologists from the University of Minnesota, Louis B. Wilson and William M. Chowning, who headed the team. Wilson and Chowning shocked both the public and the medical community by documenting eighty-eight cases that had occurred between 1895 and 1902, of which sixty-four had been fatal, establishing the terrifying mortality rate of 72.7 percent.

The pathologists explored all the newly discovered sources of disease, including water, insects, and arthropods, such as ticks and mites. Every afflicted person that Wilson and Chowning examined had been bitten by a wood tick two to eight days prior to the development of symptoms.

In 1904, with property values in the Bitterroot plummeting, the Montana State Board of Health obtained a commitment from the US surgeon general to sponsor research there until the nature of Rocky Mountain spotted fever was completely understood. But one of the effects of this commitment was to emphasize that the answers weren't known, and so, with plans for tourism, irrigation, and orchards in the works, the local press started to avoid mentioning the disease. There was humiliation and fear attached to it, so when someone died of Rocky Mountain spotted fever, the obituary writer avoided giving the cause of death, much as during the AIDS epidemic seventy years later.

The locals adopted the habit of examining their bodies nightly for ticks. Those who worked outdoors, especially on the infectious west bank of the river, also started carrying small bottles of carbolic acid with them. Carbolic acid was one of the modern miracles of the new age. The British surgeon Sir Joseph Lister, who had pioneered the idea of keeping surgery safe from dangerous microorganisms, developed carbolic acid as an antiseptic. However, if it was applied directly to the skin, which the Bitterroot people would do when they opened the bottle and held it upside down over the tick bite, a red acid welt appeared on the skin. Still, this was better than the killer fever. Not surprisingly, given the level of fear, many fraudulent medicines supposedly guaranteed to save you were sold as cures or preventatives in the Bitterroot, including sarsaparilla, an early version of root beer. This trade was much dampened in 1906 by the passage of the Pure Food and Drug Act, a piece of legislation Birdseye would one day play an important role in revising.

Also among the new fields of science was entomology, the study of insects. After 1890, when it was discovered that arthropods—eight-legged cousins of insects—could transmit disease-causing microorganisms, a wide range of doctors, public health officials, and veterinarians became interested in studying ticks. In 1909 the term *medical entomology* came into use for the specific study of the role of arthropods in disease. Therefore, the project in the Bitterroot represented the forefront of pioneering medical research, and the scientists who worked there were among the first pathologists in medical history.

Howard Taylor Ricketts, a pathologist at the University of Chicago, became interested in Rocky Mountain spotted fever, and in 1906 he went to the Bitterroot to conduct his investigations. He proved that the wood tick was the transmitter of the disease and successfully identified the organism that caused it, for which he won the dubious honor of having it named after him, *Rickettsia rickettsii*. In 1910 he went off to study an outbreak of typhus, a somewhat related disease, in Mexico and died while working on it. Field epidemiology was very dangerous work.

In February 1910 Robert Cooley, Montana's first official state entomologist, who was deeply committed to solving the Bitterroot spotted fever problem, went to Washington, D.C., to ask help from the US Biological Survey in studying the connection between wild animals and the life cycle of the tick. The survey and the US Bureau of Entomology were both housed in the same small brick building. Cooley left with three recruits: Willard V. King, a gifted entomology student from Montana who had delayed his senior year to work for the bureau; Arthur H. Howell, a thirty-eight-year-old zoologist from the survey who would publish 118 works on birds and mammals by the time he died in 1940; and Bob Birdseye, a twenty-four-year-old college dropout.

No one else had been willing to volunteer because there was no guarantee of anyone's safety. Howell was a married man with children, and he agreed to work in the field camp only on the condition that a younger volunteer, single with no children, would go trapping and shooting with him in the highly infested areas—a role that Birdseye was more than happy to assume.

To Bob's great joy, part of his job was unrestricted hunting. The age of extermination was over: A growing number of Americans believed that too many animals were being killed, and government agencies were modifying their outlook in order to manage wildlife populations and restrict the kill. However, Bob was exempt from the new restrictions, free to kill as he saw fit in the effort to collect a wide range of ticks and find a cure for spotted fever. Thrilled, he shot and trapped gophers, chipmunks, pine squirrels, woodchucks, ground squirrels, wood rats, snowshoe rabbits, cottontail rabbits, several species of mice, flying squirrels, badgers, weasels, muskrats, and bats. He also killed the large and dangerous brown bears, mountain sheep, coyotes, both mule and white-tailed deer, and elk. Most of what he killed he shot, but he also set traps. In the process he collected 4,495 ticks and killed 717 wild animals, though his goal was to get 1,000. He was Buffalo Bill at last.

The center for this science and adventure was a suitably rustic abandoned log cabin that had once been a farmhouse. Cooley, King, Birdseye, and a cook named Paul Stanton lived and did research in the cabin, which they named Camp Venustus, after the scientific name for the dangerous tick they were studying, *Dermacentor venustus*. When the men posed for a picture in front of the cabin, Stanton wore his cook's apron and the other three stood in their suits and ties. In a three-piece tweedy suit, a small man with already-thinning hair, and spectacles, Birdseye did not look that different from the famous inventor and entrepreneur he would become in his fifties. The photo gives no clue that this man risked his life every day, wandering into the canyons on horseback with his hunting rifle.

After Bob became famous, he said little about his significant contributions to the medical research or the historic significance of the project with which he had been associated. In interviews he was often asked about this period, and he always talked about how many animals he killed, sometimes pointing out that it was well over the usual limit. He would also reminisce about spending a lot of time out in the wilderness with his colleagues and playing practical jokes on one another.

Howell was often the target of pranks, as he would remain in the cabin writing a paper on their work on which only his name would appear. He'd made clear from the outset that he intended to avoid danger. Back in Washington, he'd reasoned that, since he was married with children, the job was too dangerous for him to do fieldwork. King and Birdseye had made arrangements with a nearby doctor in the event a tick infected one of them; Howell often stated that at any sign of a tick embedded on him he was packing for Washington. Bob and Willard could see that this was a young man's game out in their cabin in the foothills, where they would take all the risks, and therefore devised a clever plan.

In the cabin the three checked one another for ticks every morning and night. Bob proposed an idea to Willard that "if on one of the nightly inspections we could just discover a tick between Mr. Howell's shoulder blades where he could not possibly see that it was purely imaginary, he would be off for Washington and we could do the paper work as well as the field work." So one day, while skinning a coyote he had shot and putting the ticks he had found into vials, Bob put one tick, engorged with coyote blood, into a separate vial. At night while examining Howell, Bob claimed to find a tick between his shoulder blades. Howell was so upset, he insisted that Bob not only cut it out with a scalpel but also cauterize the wound, which Bob obligingly accomplished with a heated blade as Howell winced in pain. Then Bob handed him the vial with the tick from the coyote. It worked even better than the two young men had anticipated, for the next morning Howell was making arrangements to return to Washington.

Some weeks later Bob had a remarkable hunting trip in three days of pouring rain. He shot three wild mountain sheep, shy creatures found on inaccessible rocky ledges, and a brown bear and collected an enormous quantity of ticks from the bodies. He was so excited that he neglected to check himself for ticks, and when he finally did by an evening campfire, he found seven of them. Three were thoroughly swollen with his blood. For several days he had the aches and nausea that were well-known symptoms of spotted fever. He spent three terrified days before he realized that he simply had a grippe from being out for too many days in the rain. But it left him feeling that his joke on Howell was not as funny as he had thought it was.

Years later he told Howell what he had done, and according to Bob, Howell laughed. He had probably been relieved to return to Washington anyway.

Now the two young men, Bob and Willard, were on their own, along with the cook and occasional visits from Cooley. An unknown percentage of the tiny creatures they were gathering for study could deliver a fatal bite. A horse serum had been developed that might protect them from tick bites, but it was untested, and Bob and Willard thought the serum was as risky as facing the ticks.

While they were in the field, Josiah J. Moore, a University of Chicago pathologist, concluded from experiments that the minimum amount of time a tick needed to attach to a guinea pig in order to infect it was one hour and forty-five minutes, and that on the average it had to stay in place, feeding on the host, for ten hours. Cooley instructed Bob and Willard—in fact, it may have originally been Howell's idea—to stop their work every two hours to inspect each other's bodies for ticks. They did occasionally find a tick, but neither ever contracted spotted fever, possibly because of luck or because Moore was right about the necessary feeding time.

This procedure became standard in tick collecting for

spotted fever. So did their clothing. They wore high shoes with additional leggings tied onto the shoes and the pant legs so nothing could fly up a trouser leg. Their outer clothes, cotton for the summer weather, were soaked in kerosene, which at least for a short time served as a tick repellent. At night they left their clothes in an airtight closet with bisulfate of carbon, a common insecticide.

By day Willard went into the brush with his flag for flushing out ticks and vials for collecting them. He had a white wool flag, later replaced by lighter flannel, on a pole, and he waved it in the brush. Bob, with a hunting rifle on his shoulder and as many traps as he could carry, went out into the most infested canyons. Bob photographed the animals, and Willard photographed and studied the ticks. At night the two young men lay in their tent, having lively debates about the future of the spotted-fever campaign. Back at the cabin, Willard worked late into the night at his microscope. They wanted to document the complete life cycle of the tick and determine which animals served as hosts at which stages.

When Game Warden J. L. DeHart learned of the quantity of animals Bob had killed, he angrily referred to it as "wanton slaughter." It was perfectly legal, and the slaughter was not useless. The ticks that were collected led Willard to determine that they had a two-year life cycle, not one year, as Ricketts had thought. This was significant, because it enabled Bob to determine that the tick fed on small animals, such as mice, when it was young but as a mature adult moved to large animals. He showed that it was pointless to have a campaign against small rodents, including the gopher (correctly called Columbian ground squirrel), which had come to be regarded by the young men as the leading culprit. Bob and Willard concluded that spotted fever could be controlled only if a campaign against small rodents was combined with a program treating large animals, principally domestic livestock, with repellent.

It was an important breakthrough, but this was not what ranchers wanted to hear. They did not want the expense of treating their livestock; rather, they preferred blaming everything on the little gopher, which was, for them, a hated and destructive pest.

Cooley erected livestock dipping vats throughout the valley for ranchers to voluntarily run their cattle through. But the program was not really voluntary, because ranchers who did not dip their livestock could not move their animals. In a community that tended to be distrustful of any government programs, it only added to this one's unpopularity that it took some experimenting to get the right strength of arsenic in the dipping vats so it would kill the ticks but not hurt the livestock. Hides and udders got burned before the right formula was found. The ranchers had been much happier with Ricketts, who simply endorsed a program to exterminate gophers. In the long run, though, it became obvious that the new program was more effective.

Since there were no ticks in the winter, the project suspended activities then. In the winter of 1912 Bob was back in Washington, and he did not return to Montana. The spotted fever campaign continued without him and had its first fatality: Thomas McClintic of the US Public Health Service. In all, fourteen people died in the fight against spotted fever between 1912 and 1977. In the 1940s, with the discovery of antibiotics, a cure was found, and the crisis seemed to be over, except for another serious outbreak in the 1970s.

The research in which Birdseye participated has led to solving riddles about other serious illnesses, such as Legionnaires' disease, Lyme disease, and Potomac horse fever. It led to the opening of the second-largest government laboratory in the United States, in Hamilton, Montana, where World War II studies on insect-borne diseases helped save the lives of soldiers throughout the Pacific. If Birdseye had done nothing else, his fieldwork on spotted fever and ticks would have earned him a footnote in history, as it did Willard King, who went on to distinguish himself studying the mosquitoes that were plaguing World War II troops in New Guinea.

But Bob had a different destiny, though he had little notion of it at the time. He only knew that the century was still young and so was he, and there were opportunities for other adventures. All his life Birdseye was restless—eager to move on to the next thing. In 1912 the next thing was Labrador, a sparsely populated frozen wilderness that would give him his most famous idea.

CHAPTER FIVE

Labrador: A Frozen Land

B ob had not yet turned twenty-four when, in 1912, he was invited to spend six weeks along the Labrador coast on the hospital ship of the celebrated medical missionary Wilfred Grenfell. Bob knew he wanted to do something daring and original, and he wanted to make money doing it. And so he said good-bye again to Eleanor, the explorer's daughter, who understood his need to go, and he headed north.

Labrador was one of the most remote and undeveloped corners of the world. At the time it was a possession of Newfoundland, which was classified a dominion, a self-ruling non-nation of the British Commonwealth. Canada had a similar status but was separate from Newfoundland and its frozen northern possession.

Labrador and Newfoundland's first Europeans were fishermen, drawn there in the seventeenth century by the huge profits to be made back home selling dried and salted codfish, with which the American North Atlantic was teeming. Cod, like the buffalo and the passenger pigeon, thrived in the North American wilderness in extraordinary numbers, beyond anything Europeans had known.

Also beyond anything they'd known were the bitterly cold, long Labrador winters. Many Europeans thought the northern winters were so harsh as to make the region uninhabitable for year-round settlement—an odd assessment, since there were indigenous people living there at the time. But New England was far milder and soon had year-round settlements and even a year-round cod fishery. In Newfoundland and Labrador, on the other hand, the harbors froze up in the winter and fishing was discontinued. While a few fishermen would endure the Labrador winter, the rest would leave and return for the spring thaw. Once the harbor froze, there was no way in or out.

The European fishermen who settled in Labrador lived a life of hardship and poverty, which is why there was little interest from Labrador in separating from England in 1776; nor were Newfoundland and Labrador interested in 1849, when Canada gained self-government. When they finally did contemplate self-rule, it was as their own country and not part of "Canady," which seemed a very far-off and different place from these cold and rugged colonies. In 1907 Newfoundland gained dominion status and Labrador went with it, becoming a kind of colony of Newfoundland without representation in the legislature. It wasn't until 1949 that the two finally joined Canada.

In 1912, when Bob went to Labrador, he was going to a place far wilder than the American Wild West. Most of the 250,000 combined population of Labrador and Newfoundland consisted of fishermen in the more southern island, Newfoundland. Few people lived in Labrador through the winter, and there were no towns or cities, only a few villages.

Most Labradoreans were fishermen, huddled in the rocky coves along the coast; fur breeders, trappers, and traders; the indigenous Inuit, referred to by Europeans as Eskimos; or Montagnais Indians, who lived in small groups in the interior, descendants of the Algonquians who had been pushed north. There were animals that could be shot for meat, hides, and furs, as well as salmon, halibut, herring, lobsters, and above all, cod to be caught and eaten in the summer. In March there were seals to be hunted. Berries were the only local fruit, and the only greens were the tops of turnips in the summer. Anything else that was to be eaten, including fruits, vegetables, and grains, had to be imported in the summer months before the harbors froze.

Dogsleds provided the only winter transportation except for snowshoes for hiking. There was no electricity or telephone service. Most people made their own soap from boiling spruce ashes with seal fat. The only doctors were those who worked in the two small hospitals built by Grenfell, which unfortunately were too far for most people to reach.

Wilfred Thomason Grenfell was born in 1865 in England and attended medical school in London; however, he soon became interested in the missionary movement and spreading Christianity. At that time (the time of Bob Birdseye's birth) the British Empire was losing its power in the world. Young men were no longer recruited to fight wars to gain control of far-off lands. Many young men, raised in a tradition of going off on far-flung adventures, became missionaries.

In 1892 Grenfell was sent to Newfoundland and Labrador to continue missionary work with fishermen. When he was studying Labrador, he found an old map that said, "Labrador was discovered by the English. There is nothing in it of any value." In fact, many Englishmen saw their countrymen making fortunes on cod and furs from there and viewed Labrador and Newfoundland as sources of great wealth. But the people in Labrador who produced the salt cod and fox furs for Europe were in fact pitifully poor. They traded their products to large companies like the Hudson Bay Company in exchange for supplies and ended up in perpetual debt.

The day Grenfell first arrived, a man took him to a hovel made of sod and showed him a man dying of pneumonia. Grenfell realized that he had found the place where he was most needed.

Most of the fishermen had never seen a doctor. Grenfell wrote:

> *Deformities went untreated. The crippled and blind halted through life, victims of what "the blessed Lord saw best for them." The torture of an ingrowing toenail, which could be relieved in a few minutes, had incapacitated one poor father for years. Tuberculosis and rickets carried on their evil work unchecked. Preventable poverty was the efficient handmaid of these two latter diseases.*

The following year he built Labrador's first hospital, in Battle Harbour, a community of a few dozen dark-roofed white buildings wedged between the frozen sea and the icebound cliffs on the Atlantic coast of southern Labrador, just north of the straits that led to the mouth of the St. Lawrence River. Then he built a second—they were little more than cottages—farther up the coast, at Indian Harbour. In 1894 he formed the Grenfell Medical Mission.

At first Grenfell spent his winters, when Labrador ports were frozen and inaccessible, raising money in Britain and the United States. In 1899 his new hospital ship, the coal-fired two-masted *Strathcona I*, was launched, and starting in 1902 he spent every other winter in Labrador. He learned to love the Labrador winter in the same way Bob Birdseye would learn to love it: for its stark beauty, the thrill and fun of dog-sledding, the simplicity of life without stores or crowds, and the warmth of the rare encounters with the few comrades who were spending the winter the same way. Grenfell wrote that, because of the absence of stores, "we are relieved of the constant suggestion that we need something."

Once spring came he was on his hospital ship, bringing medical help, sailing into the Labrador coast's deep unknown fjords and islands, some of which had never been charted on a map. It was such a six-week tour that Bob joined in the spring of 1912 as the harbors thawed and became navigable again. The older man had a huge impact on Bob. Though Grenfell never mentioned him in his 1919 autobiography, Birdseye frequently referred to Grenfell in his journals.

At the age of forty-nine, with his bushy mustache and smiling eyes, Grenfell was an adventurer, forever trying out new ideas. He experimented with bringing in reindeer from Lapland as domestic animals that could haul goods like sled dogs. He also started a cooperative so the local people could buy provisions at reasonable prices.

Grenfell understood that the root of the health problems there was poverty, and the root of that poverty was that the natives were being forced to trade what they produced to the big companies for the things they needed instead of earning money. He was constantly looking for more profitable ways of working in which the locals could earn cash. Instead of trapping foxes for their furs, which they then traded, he thought they could farm the foxes and sell their pups. It had never been done in Labrador, but Grenfell thought it not only had the potential of earning the locals a considerable amount of cash but was more humane than letting foxes starve to death with a leg in the steel jaw of a trap. He knew nothing about the breeding of foxes but was confident that it was feasible because he had seen a litter at the Washington zoo that had been born in captivity.

Grenfell established a farm in St. Anthony, a handful of scattered houses in northern Newfoundland. The village had one of the harshest climates in the region but was a convenient location because he had a hospital there. He brought the foxes in from Labrador on his ship, and a visiting Harvard scholar recalled the frisky pups playing on deck with dogs and people. The red foxes were particularly friendly and would run up to greet visitors. The white-and-silvers were shyer. But foxes were difficult to breed; it was hard to keep the young alive, and after a few years some that had become favorite pets died of a spreading disease. Grenfell closed down the project and turned the farm into a summer vegetable garden.

● ● ●

Where others saw only wilderness, Bob saw hidden opportunity. When Grenfell talked about fox farming, it caught his interest. Birdseye had made money in coyote furs in the Southwest, and animals were something with which he was experienced. He had decided, perhaps in the Bitterroot project, that, as he later put it, he "was not cut out for a career in pure science and wanted to get into some field where I could apply scientific knowledge to an economic opportunity."

A successful fox farm had been established in the interior of Labrador by the time Birdseye arrived. Fox farming had become the most important industry on Prince Edward Island, with high prices being paid for live foxes. At every port where the *Strathcona* landed, Bob talked to fur traders and other men involved with foxes, and he concluded that there was money to be made in trapping silver foxes and shipping them to the United States as breeding stock.

By July of 1912 Birdseye was back in New York, looking for an investor in his new scheme. According to his journal, his father wrote a letter to Harris Hammond, a wealthy contact in Gloucester, Massachusetts, which is the earliest record of a link between Birdseye and the New England city. The Hammond family spent part of their time there. Harris was the son of John Hays Hammond, a wealthy mining engineer who had worked in Mexico and South Africa. The elder Hammond was a close friend of the president of the United States and later Supreme Court Justice William Howard Taft and many other well-placed men. When John Hays Hammond Jr. said he wanted to be an inventor, his father had the boy sit down with Thomas Edison and Alexander Graham Bell to talk about his ideas. John's older brother Harris was more in the mold of his father. He understood about adventures.

Birdseye had a difficult time getting a meeting with Hammond. He tried visiting the businessman's office day after day. When finally they did meet, Bob explained his idea of fox farming in broad terms. Hammond asked few questions and sought no details. He agreed to give the venture some backing, handed Bob a check for $750—the equivalent of about $18,000 today—to get him started, and told Birdseye, "Keep me informed." This was the beginning of the Hammond and Birdseye Fur Company.

The next day Bob spent $350 on supplies and deposited the remaining $400 in a bank in St. John's, the Newfoundland capital. It would take thousands of dollars to buy enough animals to start breeding foxes. Birdseye later said that he also got backing from Grenfell's New York connections.

Bob bought an abandoned fur-trading outpost in Labrador 250 miles up the coast from Battle Harbour, where the ships came in from Newfoundland. That is a long way from town when the only transportation is dogsleds. In St. John's, learning that there was a proposal to ban the export of foxes, he met with legislators to try to dissuade them from the measure. He finally found his loophole, as there was to be no ban on the export of locally raised offspring.

But before he could raise foxes, he needed knowledge and skills. He studied the farms on Prince Edward Island and drew detailed diagrams. He then obtained a license to capture wild foxes for breeding. He also met with the fishing commissioner and other officials, went to shops, and visited a seal factory. On his crossing to Labrador he met fishermen and grilled them about their techniques and their problems. He operated like a journalist, constantly hunting down information.

He learned that foxes died easily, even from drinking too much milk, and puppies were even more fragile. They could eat cod heads, which were virtually free, and "moldy bread was good fox feed [too]. Fish in seal oil was cheap, kept well through the winter and was a good feed. Liver tends to loosen foxes' bowels. For breeding one male can serve two females although it took experience to accomplish this—that is, on the part of the breeder."

When Bob got to Prince Edward Island, breeding foxes were selling for as much as $8,000. He was able to find three pairs to begin with, which he bought for only $1,000 a pair. He seemed fond of the animals, describing some as playful, some, especially females, as gentle. They seemed almost like pets, if you didn't contemplate their fate. He wrote, "Considering that the foxes are supposed to be wild, they aren't at all bashful any longer." The problem was that they were constantly dying, especially new pups.

In addition to learning the intricacies of breeding and raising wild foxes, Bob had to learn how to survive a Labrador winter. Clothing, for example, had to be heavy enough to hold in his body heat and yet light enough to keep him from sweating; if he sweat, it would freeze, especially at night.

He also had to learn about sleds and sled dogs and managing a team. Birdseye was impressed with "the full-blood husky dog of northern Labrador," he wrote in his journal, and he referred to the huskies' howling as "canine music." After listening to them through a sleepless night, he wrote that it reminded him of the noise made by a large crowd on election night.

Labrador sled dogs were close to wolves in appearance and often in temperament. These were extremely strong dogs, fearless and ready to attack whatever threatened, even a polar bear or a man, both of which a real wolf would shy away from. They seemed impervious to cold, even when covered in ice. They could save a man's life, because they could always find their way, even when snow blindness or fog bewildered the human driver. They averaged about six miles an hour but were capable of traveling at two or three times that speed. Each dog had its unique personality and temperament, and a driver needed to know his dogs.

The sled, the *komatik*, was designed for hauling freight for scientific expeditions and for traders. It was very different from the Alaskan racing sled, with the perch in the back, that most people picture as a dogsled. A *komatik* was an eleven-foot-long platform on long runners, ideally made of light and durable black spruce, although there were many variations. There were even stories of drivers in an emergency breakdown finding whale ribs to use. The runners should be slightly more than two feet apart. Packing a *komatik* required skill. It was extremely important that the weight be right for the terrain and that the freight be well balanced.

Bob traveled all over Labrador by dogsled. On January 10, 1913, he averaged almost ten miles an hour, covering sixty-five miles in six and a half hours, which is the total amount of daylight in Labrador at that time of year. His journal shows him frequently gone for three or sometimes even six weeks, procuring foxes or provisions. He often wrote of six-hour journeys just to visit a neighbor. Surviving the weather was challenging. It was often well below zero degrees Fahrenheit, sometimes as low as −40 degrees. He later said that he regularly suffered from frostbite. "After a while you get used to it just like mosquito bites."

Provisioning a journey was important, since there was always a possibility of spending some extra time lost. The *komatik* traveler had to know what kind of provisions to take; that salted food, such as pork or cod, resisted freezing and was therefore better than canned food, which would quickly freeze up and would be very difficult to thaw and also had extra inedible weight. Grenfell liked to travel with "pork buns"—heavy dark buns laced with salt pork and molasses, so dense that one of them was as filling as a meal. Bob lived on these buns when traveling with his dog team.

More is known about Bob Birdseye in his five years in Labrador than at any other time in his life, partly because this was the time he most liked to talk about, but mainly because he filled long evenings alone by writing page after page of mail to his family, even though the mail-carrying ships could not get past the ice for the entire winter and much of the spring. In 1914 the ice did not melt enough for ships to arrive until July. But Bob kept writing and sent off a thick pile of pages when he had a chance. Despite his wanderlust, he felt close to his family and missed them.

• • •

Bob's journals show a lonely man who relished time spent with others, none more than Grenfell, whom he always referred to as Dr. Grenfell. "Golly it was so good to see him again," Birdseye wrote to his family after the Englishman visited him in the summer of 1914. "He is certainly a Prince, and it is one big life-size pleasure to meet him."

He also kept what he called field journals. It is not certain exactly why he kept them. The name implies a scientific purpose. It may have had something to do with his training as a biologist or his work with the US Biological Survey. But the style, tone, and even content of these journals (indices and accounting aside) were not very different from the letters he wrote home. They read as though he were chatting with someone.

The journals were handwritten in bound hardcover doeskin notebooks with lined pages. He started the first one during his last summer in Montana and continued the practice in Labrador until his final entry in the twelfth notebook in July 1916.

The letters and notebooks tell much about Bob Birdseye, even though he did not readily talk about emotions or matters of the heart. Descriptions of his visits to fox farmers on Prince Edward Island show that he made very quick assessments of other people. He wanted to learn from anyone he encountered and noted in his journal who was forthcoming and from whom he had to "wile" the information.

The journals show that he was an extremely methodical man and a tireless worker. In the early notebooks he numbered each page and used the last pages for a detailed index. In later notebooks the index was dropped and the final pages were devoted to a detailed accounting of his expenses. After his first winter he realized that he needed help, someone to run his fox farm while he was away on trips, and he brought in a recruit from his hometown of Montclair, Perry W. Terhune. The fact that one of Terhune's tasks while Birdseye was away was maintaining his field journal shows that he was keeping journals as more than just a personal record. The parts written by Terhune are in a much more careless script, with no descriptions, no index, and many days skipped or simply marked "No work done." Bob never had such days. He worked on writing or indexing the journals, checked accounts, or spent the day reading, but he always reported some profitable use of his time.

The writings show that he had a self-effacing, sometimes corny, but endearing sense of humor. He wrote to his family, "Wouldn't you folks welcome a rest from this long-winded journal, and a few weeks of 'I am well! I am warm!' 'I am sleepy,' 'I have a frozen toe,' 'I went to Cartwright and frost burned my nose'?"

Normally Bob liked to describe the food he was eating. In a letter to his parents he wrote about rabbit, "Mostly we had 'um fried! But there's a scattered pie, and an occasional stew. One of the favorite breakfasts is fried rabbit livers, the thinnest crispiest deliciousest bacon, hot cornbread, and powerful good coffee. Doesn't that sound good?"

If Bob were alive today, he would be called a foodie, someone who spent much of his time thinking about food, cooking food, and eating food. He seemed obsessed with the subject. Of course, food was, as he frequently pointed out, a matter of survival. "Weather and Grub!" he once wrote.

"Those are the two fundamental facts on which every other event hinges in this neck of the woods—or rather barrens."

In his journals and letters he frequently offered recipes, and these included not only local game and fish dishes but also desserts:

MOLASSES PIE

For dinner today we had my first molasses pie—and it was really mighty good. It was between two crusts. No other flavoring than molasses was used but Mrs. Lewis says that boiling the molasses and adding a few spices improves the flavor of the pie.

He would frequently end a recipe with an editorial comment such as "Yum! Yum!"

He often wrote in either his journal or his letters home what he ate for breakfast or dinner. The entry on October 13, 1914, was a typical one, when he sat down at his fox farm and began a letter to his family:

Well, folks, having just disposed of some toast and cocoa after a ten-mile ante breakfast walk from Cartwright in a roundabout way to Muddy Bay, I feel in good humor to inflict another chapter of this letter.

And as was always his style, the more exotic the food, the more enthusiastically he received it. His palate, like his mind, was endlessly curious. He wrote his parents that a porcupine he had eaten was "unexpectedly tender, in spite of the beast's age and sex." He described as the "pièce de résistance" of "one of the most scrumptious meals I ever ate" lynx that had marinated for an entire month in sherry and was then stewed and served with a sauce made from the marinade. He said he ate polar bear and professed a particular fondness for the front half of a skunk.

Birdseye loved seal meat, especially that of the ringed seal, which he correctly identified as *Phoca hispida*, except for old males. He wrote his family, "'orned Howl (horned-owl) for Sunday dinner—does that sound good? Well, it *was* good, no matter how it sounds." He also ate beaver and a variety of birds, including hawks. He explained to his family that he was able to eat fresh meat every day by having "no food prejudices" and eating "anything that tastes good." He was so enthusiastic about these foods that he threatened to can some of them and bring them back to New Jersey "so you folks could sample them."

He even studied local books to learn about food traditions and was very excited when a book at GM explained the English origin of the Labradorean tradition of eating pea soup on Saturday nights.

The writings also show that he was endlessly resourceful. He fashioned a berry harvester from a tin can and repaired engines. He had already become a professional hunter, but now he also became a skilled fisherman, catching salmon and trout on the fly, jigging for cod, netting capelin.

In October 1912 he went goose hunting with Grenfell, also an avid sportsman, and Grenfell laughed at what a voracious hunter Bob was, even drawing an ink illustration in Bob's journal of the bespectacled Birdseye stomping through the marsh with his shotgun stock held high, trying to club a fleeing bird. Some have attributed this drawing to Bob, since it was in his journal, but it bears Grenfell's initials, WTG, and matches the style of the doctor's other drawings.

Bob also learned medical skills from assisting Grenfell. He described an operation where Grenfell successfully removed a second thumb from a six-month-old child's hand. Grenfell had enough confidence in his young friend that he left medicines with him, and apparently Birdseye did give medical assistance to locals during the winters. He recorded having treated some two dozen patients with such complaints as sore throats, toothaches, pain in the side, and hacking cough.

In Birdseye's Labrador writings are some early signs of the inventor. One day in early 1915 he was at a house with a tub and got to take a bath. He wrote that when he got back to New Jersey, he should invent a foldable rubber tub for traveling. There is no trace of his ever having built it.

From time to time, living in a frozen world, he turned his mind to reflecting on the nature of freezing itself. In December 1914 he made a simple observation that tortured and plagued his curiosity for years. He wrote his father:

> *Practically every morning throughout the winter the water in my pitcher is frozen—often so hard that it has to be thawed out with hot water. So a few mornings ago, after a cold night, I was much surprised to find, upon thrusting a hand into the pitcher, to find it filled with water instead of ice. When, however, I poured some of the water into my*

bowl and some more into a glass, and then scooped
up a handful I found that the bowl was full of a
spongy mass of ice crystals; and the same formation
had taken place in the glass and the water pitcher—
yet a few seconds before there had been no sign of
ice in the water. Evidently the water had been in a
state of equilibrium—at the freezing point, and all
ready to congeal, but needing some little stirring up
to start the crystallization. I seem to remember seeing
the same thing done in a physics lab experiment,
but certainly never ran across it before "in nature."
Did you?

Some days later he commented on the phenomenon to his family again, adding, "Some of you physics-sharks please give me an explanation of this happening." This is the earliest record of Bob contemplating the science of freezing and the laws of crystallization.

In Labrador he still seemed to be searching for his career, but he already was drawn to the idea of having numerous careers, something he took great pride in later. Toward the end of his life he liked to tell the story that a young man once asked him if he had it to do over, would he choose the same occupation. His answer was "Which occupation?"

Photography was one of the new fields he often considered. When he first arrived, after less than a week there, he shipped out his first six rolls of film. The locals loved to pose for pictures and would ask him, "Would you sketch off me?" (Would you take my picture?) That first year Bob had the idea of a book of photographs on Labrador. In July 1913, when in New York, he dropped off a proposal with photos at Scribner's. He never commented on the publisher's response, but no book deal was forthcoming. On September 5, in St. John's, Newfoundland, Bob sold twenty-five prints to a publisher to be used in a picture book on Labrador. He sold the prints for $1 each and retained all future rights. Bob was always smart about business agreements.

He also seemed interested in writing, perhaps influenced by Grenfell, who wrote and published engaging tales of the people he met in Labrador. Bob's father and his sister Miriam were regularly publishing books, though neither his father's legal books nor his sister's books on nutrition seemed destined for a wide audience. In November 1913 *Outing*, a sportsmen's magazine from Chicago, published an article by Birdseye titled "Camping in a Labrador-hole," about an incident that had happened a year earlier. The style was not unlike that of his journals, regularly stopping to tell readers what he ate. He described how difficult it was to manage a dog team and to travel by sled, and how they were trapped in a snow blizzard for three days with nothing to eat but raisins, prunes, rice, and the candy he always carried to give to children. The experience was nearly an early end to Bob Birdseye, and in fact five of his dogs did not survive. The writing lacked a strong storytelling narrative but was illustrated with his photos, his admiral-in-sealskins self-portrait, and shots of his sled and dog team.

A month later *Outing* came out with another article of his, titled "The Truth About Fox Farming." This was more like the Birdseye known in later years: everything you could know about fox farming, complete with his diagrams and, of course, a few photos taken by him of his and other fox farms. His photography was without artifice, intended purely to document. It was a new skill for him, but at this time there were not many amateur photographers, so he was a pioneer.

In 1913 Bob went back for a visit to Montclair. That summer, between lunches with his brother Kellogg, visits to his father's office, meetings with backer Harris Hammond, consultations with furriers, a visit to Scribner's with his book proposal, and even a visit to Amherst—all of which were mentioned in his journal—Bob probably managed to see Eleanor in Washington or New York, but he mentioned nothing of this in his journal. By August 28 he was back in Newfoundland, preparing for Labrador's early winter.

The following year he visited home again. It seemed almost certain that summer in 1914 that Europe was about to go to war, what history would later call World War I. This had huge implications for Birdseye's fox business. For one thing, he got his cash flow from British investors, possibly Grenfell connections. He wrote in his journal, "Because of the war possibly causing some of the pledged English underscriptions to be withdrawn we might get into serious straights [sic], for want of capital." The other reason a war would affect Bob's business was that the primary market for fox fur was Europe. American women seldom wore such furs. It was a European look, and Europe was about to be consumed with war. The principal fur centers, in London and Leipzig, were both shutting down. The Hudson Bay Company stopped buying fur.

After two years in which he traveled, by his estimate,

five thousand miles by dogsled gathering foxes, in 1914 Bob's business was shut down by the Newfoundland government, which finally banned the export of live foxes from Labrador and Newfoundland. The conventional wisdom of the time was that the high-quality-fur business was dying.

The fur market in New York was dismal. Top-quality ermines were selling for 15 cents each. But Bob saw opportunity. The United States, the one developed country that was not at war, was prospering. Surely this new prosperity would be reflected in fashionable women in furs, especially with pelts available for bargain prices. This was Bob's kind of gamble, and he had an advantage, as he was a great salesman. His obvious intelligence, his ability to articulate his idea, and his contagious enthusiasm almost always carried him through. He persuaded a New York furrier to stake him to $8,000.

Back in Labrador Bob began killing his foxes, freezing them by packing them in snow, and sending them to be skinned. He also started buying quality pelts wherever he could find them at cut-rate prices. He traveled thousands of miles by dogsled again, buying furs, offering low prices but paying in cash. The big fur buyers rarely offered cash, so he was able to make very good deals. Labradoreans were selling their furs for historically low prices. He wrote of how he bought one top-quality silver fox for $375 that a year before would have been worth $4,000.

He wrote that the people were so hard up, they would take "any price I see fit to give." He did express some remorse for exploiting poor and desperate people, even commenting on how badly dressed their children were, with leaky boots. But he didn't change his behavior, pointing out that he was still paying "twice what the Hudson Bay Company is giving." By the end of 1914 he had cornered the fur market and cleared $6,000 profit—almost $140,000 in today's money.

With these substantial earnings he felt ready to marry the woman he loved. In July 1915 Bob left Labrador, and in St. John's he wired home to say he was coming. According to his journal, he also "wired EG." That small notation was the first time he ever mentioned Eleanor Gannett in his journal.

On July 25, 1915, Bob was back in New Jersey. That night he sat down with his older brother Kellogg to discuss business and told him that he was engaged to marry Eleanor. In his journal he wrote that he told Kellogg about "EG"—it was almost as though he didn't want her to be identified by anyone except himself.

Then, for almost an entire month, there are no entries in his journal, but he was not lonely. On August 29 he returned with Eleanor by car from Berlin, New York. In his journal he described the Taconic Inn, where they stayed, the various people on the property, and who their families were. He included in the journal the torn upper half of two pieces of letterhead with a picture of the Taconic Inn, which boasted electric lights and steam heat. Saving these and pressing them in his journal was, for Bob, a rare sentimental gesture. But why not? Though he never mentioned it, this was his honeymoon. He also didn't mention that a week earlier, on August 21, they were married. But at least he now started referring to Eleanor in the journal by her name rather than EG.

Life had now changed, because he was married to Eleanor. Suddenly the preparations for returning to Labrador included not only the usual shopping for shotguns, ammunition, and equipment but a week of daily shopping at Wanamaker's, where day after day Eleanor and Bob's sister Miriam bought bedroom and dining room furniture, plus a great deal of aluminum and white agate kitchenware—all to be shipped to Labrador. However, New York was no longer just about business. They all went to the Museum of Natural History together and then to their first movie, *Birth of a Nation*.

Miriam seems the sibling with whom Bob had the most in common, as she was also fascinated with food. At the time she was lecturing at Cornell University on nutrition, particularly about meat. She seemed to become closer upon his marriage to Eleanor. They were both college-educated women and coincidentally would both later write about gardening.

Then Bob and Eleanor were off to Labrador by the usual route: a train to Boston; a second train to Maine; a boat to Halifax, Nova Scotia; a third train to Sydney, on Cape Breton Island; a second boat to the tiny seaport of Port aux Basques, Newfoundland; and a fourth train across the rock-bound, barely populated wild interior to St. John's before boarding one final boat to Labrador. One takes the same route today, except that the train from Port aux Basques to St. John's, which used to be called the *Newfie Bullet*, no longer runs. There is now a highway with signs warning of the perils of crossing moose.

The newlyweds had to wait two weeks at a hotel in St. John's for the boat to Labrador. Compared to anything in Labrador, St. John's was a big city, but in fact it was just a rugged fishing town, dating back to before 1620.

In October they got to Labrador and started building a new house he would name Wyndiecote, the old Long Island name that to Bob meant home. He wrote that he was spending all his time on this project. Perched on a rock ledge over Muddy Bay and reachable only by a long stairway that climbed the rocks, it was a simple house, though luxurious compared with the shacks most people lived in around the bay. Built by a local trapper, Charles Bird, it was only one story with just three rooms; windows looking out at the angry sea, the windblown sky, and distant woods surrounded the large living room. It was not an impressive structure, but it still stands today, though its location has changed. Not even Bob realized it at the time, but it is technically the birthplace of the modern frozen-food industry. It has not been preserved for its historic importance, however. It's lasted because houses are scarce in Labrador, and you don't throw away a solid one.

They finally moved in on December 9, which happened to be Bob's twenty-ninth birthday. They had hired a live-in maid—not uncommon at the time—back where they came from. Bob now took Sundays off, and he and Eleanor read and went for walks in snowshoes in −14-degree temperatures.

Eleanor, in some ways a prim and proper woman of her time, was also quite unusual, as she was ready for adventure at any time. She traveled with Bob on long journeys with a nine-dog sled, setting traps in subzero weather. Years later she liked to amuse her children with a story of the time she fell off the back of a *komatik*, and Bob, up front managing the dog team, didn't notice for about ten minutes, in which time he'd covered about a mile. He looked back and saw no Eleanor, then turned around and found her.

Eleanor adapted quickly to life on the frontier. They took

target practice together with .22 Colt revolvers, which they also used to shoot rabbits that were caught in their traps. At first, though she did well with targets, Eleanor couldn't hit the rabbits, but she soon caught on. She gradually found her place with the Hammond and Birdseye Fur Company, doing paperwork and looking after foxes, which they were still breeding, though they could export them only if they killed them. She also established a darkroom in the new house so they could develop film and make prints from Bob's photography.

In May fox pups were born. The journal, and apparently their lives, became consumed with caring for one struggling pup. Bob records when the pup gets his first teeth and when he has "a copious movement" due to the use of castor oil. Finally, on May 18, 1916, Bob reported that the pup died at 6:00 a.m. of acute indigestion.

Everyone in Labrador was eager for news of the war, which was scarce. They would not hear about it until the harbor thawed a month later. The Dominion of Newfoundland had given more than its share to the war effort: an entire regiment was slaughtered on the first day of the battle of the Somme in 1916.

In the meantime, Bob and Eleanor had foxes to worry about. Once the harbors thawed, they went back to New York. Eleanor was more than six months pregnant, but this was the soonest they could leave. Her pregnancy had not taken up nearly the space in the journal that the fox pup had. Once in New York, Birdseye simply noted, "Shortly after breakfast E and I went to Dr. Stern's office and made arrangements. I gave him carte blanche in making hospital and all other necessary arrangements." That taken care of, Bob tried to work on business in New York. After numerous attempts to meet with Hammond, who seemed always to be in Gloucester, Massachusetts, Birdseye was informed, "Mr. Hammond is no longer interested in Hammond and Birdseye." Bob's father tried to set him up with other prospective investors, and apparently something worked, because he went back to Labrador, where he awaited the arrival of Eleanor and their new baby.

On September 6, 1916, their son Kellogg was born. Five weeks later, Eleanor set off for Labrador with the baby. The ship she was to have sailed on from Newfoundland never arrived, because a German U-boat had sunk it. Finally she managed to get on the last boat for Labrador before ice shut the ports for the winter, and it had to sail through a storm to get there in time. To raise a baby in a subarctic wilderness with the closest medical facility, Grenfell's hospital in Battle Harbour, 250 miles away by dogsled seemed a risky decision. But Eleanor and Bob were not troubled by it. Years later the family would ask, "But what if Kellogg got sick?" and Eleanor would smile softly and say, "But he never did."

The first obvious change now that Bob was a father was that he stopped writing. He dropped his journals altogether and wrote far less to his family. The family would still hear from him whenever there was a mail ship, but the packets were much lighter. He urged his parents to keep writing back "the same number of good letters that you always sent me when I was a poor forlorn bachelor." Though he was always understated in his mentions of Eleanor, it was clear how much he enjoyed having her with him. He described her as "the only genuine Washingtonian north of the forty-nine." Eleanor began writing to Bob's parents, too.

FOOD IN LABRADOR

Typical of Birdseye, he did not worry a great deal about the proximity of a hospital, although he was concerned that Kellogg eat well. Ringing in his ears was Grenfell's constant admonition to the people of Labrador that it was poor diet that was causing widespread anemia, dyspepsia, beriberi, and scurvy. Fruits and vegetables had to be brought in on trips to Newfoundland. Livestock for meat or milk could not be kept, because the dogs would kill them. Sled dogs, the only means of transportation, were not optional. Now Bob thought a lot about food preservation because of the long winters. He had to have food for his family.

Fish was the cheapest, most plentiful food. One of the summer tasks was to preserve salted fish. In the winter fish was frozen by a technique called snow packing, in which food was buried in a barrel of snow and left outdoors. Since the temperature was below freezing all winter, it remained frozen until unpacked for use.

Birdseye asked himself many questions about food and survival in the subarctic. Why, he wondered, did people in Labrador eat lean food in the summer but a tremendous amount of fat in the winter? The ultimate winter survival dish was something called bruise, a combination of dried and salted food mixed with a tremendous amount of fat. Usually it was salt cod, hardtack, flour, and water, baked hard and mixed with cubed salt pork and then boiled and served like a hash with huge globs of melted pork fat. Bowls of melted fat were often placed on the table to spoon onto food. Bob laughed when he heard a host say, "Have some more grease on your bruise," but everyone then took a few spoonfuls. It was a Sunday-morning breakfast favorite. He remembered that people also ate a great deal of grease in the Southwest, where it was hot in the summer; they would open a can of corn and eat it with pork fat.

Bob reflected on such phenomena. He asked his parents in a letter why people in hot and cold climates eat more fat than those living in a temperate zone.

The constant diet of grease and preserved and conserved food gave him a longing for food that tasted fresh. "Good lord," he once wrote his family. "How fine gull gravy tastes when one hadn't had anything fresh for a long time." It was not only Bob who felt this yearning for fresh food. He told his parents that whenever people met in Labrador, the first thing they asked each other was whether they had seen any fresh food where they came from. He often described the excitement and relish with which neighbors would gather for a meal when they had gotten some fresh food. When he bought foxes, he also tried to buy beaver, lynx, martin, otter—whatever he could get. He wanted them with the furs on so he could stuff them and sell them as specimens. But also he wanted to eat the fresh meat. Everyone in Labrador craved fresh food in the winter. Although Birdseye loved irony, he was absolutely serious when he referred to a meal with fresh food as "today's big event."

His food concerns were immediate. He was not thinking

of ambitious plans to launch a new food industry; he was just trying to make sure his young son and his wife ate well. Making that task even more difficult, Bob was reluctant to travel and leave Eleanor and Kellogg alone. He wrote in a 1917 letter, "Pulling teeth would have been a mild process compared to running off and leaving E. and Sonny."

Bob and Eleanor had brought live hens with them from Newfoundland, along with a large supply of fresh potatoes, turnips, beets, carrots, parsnips, cabbages, onions, apples, and grapes. They'd also brought thirty dozen eggs, because they didn't think the Rhode Island Reds would start laying until spring. Finally, they'd brought two beef hindquarters and a whole lamb.

"So you see that our larder is going to be well-stocked," Bob wrote home to New Jersey, "and we needn't fear scurvy or rickets, or pip, or beriberi or any of those little ailments which come of a too salt diet!"

All he had to do now was figure out how to keep this trove in reasonably fresh condition throughout a long winter. In the event of failure, they also shipped a large supply of canned fruits and vegetables. The grapes froze on the way to Sandwich Bay, and the eggs spoiled quickly and could not even be fed to the foxes. But by the following spring the hens were producing. Bob had several hundred partridges frozen in the fall. Another reason that freezing, by packing snow into barrels, became more important with Eleanor's arrival was that she disliked gamey-tasting meat, so a wild goose or a partridge kept even a few days was too gamey for her.

All of this was driving Bob's lively mind to reflect on the

science of freezing. Freezing was not new. Frozen food had been available all his life. But when it thawed, it was mushy and less appealing than even canned food. Frozen food was a last resort. No one really wanted to eat it.

But to Birdseye's surprise, the frozen food in Labrador was not unpleasant. In fact, in his judgment it tasted just like fresh food. What accounted for the difference? The Inuit had traditionally enjoyed this high-quality frozen food. They fished in holes in the ice and pulled out a trout, and it instantly froze in the 30-degrees-below-zero air. When they cooked it, it tasted like fresh fish. In fact, sometimes they would put the frozen fish in water to thaw, and the fish would start swimming, still alive—according to Birdseye, sometimes after being frozen for months. Bob never understood the mystery of the live frozen fish, but he did learn to ice-fish, instantly freeze the fish in the air, store it outside in the cold, and thaw it in water when ready to cook it. And he learned to snow-pack fresh meat. Frozen game was so fresh when it thawed that it did not taste in the least aged, and even Eleanor liked it.

He noticed that the meat and fish were not as good when frozen in the early or late winter, and he wondered why. He would cut paper-thin slices of the frozen food and see that the food that had been frozen then did not have the same texture as the food frozen in the dead of winter. The spring and fall food had a grainier texture and leaked juices when thawed.

Birdseye thought about the difference between the frozen food in Labrador and commercially frozen food, with its grainy texture and leaking juices, and he realized that the ice crystals were too big. If food is frozen too slowly, the larger ice crystals will damage the cellular structure, even break down cells. Everyone knew that the height of winter was the best freezing season. Birdseye figured out why.

It was clear that in the dead of winter, when the air was −30 degrees Fahrenheit or even colder, the food froze instantly, whereas in warmer weather it took longer. This was not hard for Birdseye to understand when he thought about it: it had to do with the science of crystallization, of which everyone in Labrador had some knowledge, because preserving food with salt was a way of life there. Salting food and freezing food are opposites. For the best results, freezing needs small crystals and salting needs large ones. For centuries sea salt had been in great demand in places like Labrador that have a great deal of fish but not a sunny enough climate for evaporating seawater in the sun—the only economically viable way to produce sea salt, as the cost of fuel made cooking it down not feasible. The fish required sea salt, not because, like the fish, it came from the sea, but because of its large crystals. Solar evaporation is a very slow way to make salt, and so the crystals are very large. This is the rule with any kind of crystallization: The more slowly the crystals form, the larger they are.

He started experimenting with vegetables. He had bought a lot of cabbage in Newfoundland and had been storing it in the house. When the weather turned very cold, he took a large barrel and put an inch of seawater at the bottom. Then he put a thin layer of cabbage leaves. Once this was frozen, he added another layer of seawater and another layer of cabbage. He repeated this until he had a full barrel. When he wanted some cabbage for the family, he would lop off a chunk with an axe and cook it, and he found that it tasted exactly like cooked fresh cabbage.

Not all attempts were successful. Some caribou were butchered and frozen into blocks of ice, only to find out months later that it had not been frozen enough and the meat had rotted.

On April 6, 1917, the United States entered World War I, despite President Woodrow Wilson's election-campaign promise not to. Bob always said that he returned to the United States because of the war. But he did not clarify why.

Did they go home because of serious family problems? In May 1917 Bob's father, Clarence, and older brother Kellogg were arrested and charged with conspiracy to commit fraud. Bob had seldom taken an important step without consulting both of them. During the years he traded furs in Labrador, they had been his regular advisors and the two family members most often mentioned in his writings. And of course Bob and Eleanor had named their first son after Kellogg.

Accounts of the trial make clear that this was not a small oversight or a slight brush with the law but an elaborate conspiracy to steal a fortune. It appeared that Bob's father, a leading figure in New York State law, whose books were studied by law students and lawyers, was the ringleader in a scheme involving lying to and deceiving a considerable number of business associates, many of whom testified against him.

Whether or not this was a factor in Bob's return to the United States is not known. It may have just felt like the right time to go home. All his life Bob lost patience with a project once it succeeded, and he now had financial success as a fox breeder. It was time for a different kind of life. He was married and a father, and he intended to have more children. Their second child, Ruth, was born in 1918.

It is tempting to say that after years of contemplating freezing, making frozen food, and searching for commercial opportunities, Bob was ready to go home and start the frozen-food industry. But in fact, nothing was further from his thoughts. Back home no one liked frozen food or wanted it, and it seemed that in a temperate climate with year-round ports and a steady supply of fresh food most of the year, there was no need to freeze food. He thought his days of freezing food, just like his days of traveling by dogsled, were over. He later said of what he had learned about freezing, "I tucked this knowledge away in my subconscious mind, but its commercial possibilities did not dawn on me at that time."

CHAPTER SIX

A Very Big Idea

Bob and Eleanor and young Kellogg and Ruth, the new baby, did not settle in New York or New Jersey to be by the troubled relatives. Instead they went back to Washington, D.C., where Bob looked for a job that he would like. First he worked for Stone and Webster, a Massachusetts-based engineering and construction company with which Bob's Wall Street uncle, Henry Ebenezer, had a business involvement. Then, in 1919, Bob left this growing firm for a position as an assistant purchasing agent for the US Housing Corporation. For a time he also worked for a bottled-water producer. The life of adventure seemed well behind him in 1920, when he switched jobs again and became the assistant to the president of the US Fisheries Association, a lobbying group for commercial fishermen.

On March 5 Bob's father and brother were sentenced to two years in prison for insurance fraud. Their sentencing was covered in the *New York Times*. Clarence Frank Birdseye Sr. was a powerful, well-respected man and patriarch of the family. On April 30, 1920, Bob's father, age sixty-five, was received at the Western State Penitentiary in Pittsburgh, and became prisoner no. 10849. His occupation was given as lawyer/author. He surrendered his gold cuff links, gold collar buttons, gold penknife, and gold ring and began his sentence.

His father's and brother's convictions must have been devastating to Bob. In fact, the incident is not well known among his descendants. His father served his two years and was released in 1922 but died five years later at the age of seventy-three—two years too soon to see his namesake son become wealthy and famous. Bob's mother, Ada, moved in with Miriam in Washington, D.C., where Miriam did nutritional studies for the US Department of Agriculture. But by then Bob and Eleanor had left Washington.

Those years while his father was in prison, 1920 to 1922, were formative years for Bob Birdseye. As assistant to the president of the Fisheries Association he was confronted with the full range of fishery issues, from sea to market. He was back with the two topics that always drove his interest, wildlife and food, and the big question was how to get fish to market in better condition.

Most fish lost much of its value while being transported. "The inefficiency and lack of sanitation in the distribution of whole fresh fish so disgusted me," Bob explained twenty years later, "that I set out to develop a method which would permit the removal of inedible waste from perishable foods at production points, packaging them in compact and convenient containers, and distributing them to the housewife with their intrinsic freshness intact."

This was the beginning of what grew into a very big idea. In most markets the fish that was being sold to consumers was greatly inferior to fish landed at the docks of fishing ports. This created two problems, both of which disturbed Bob: people were not eating fish at its best, and fish was losing value on its way to the market. Bob thought that if he could find a way to deliver it to the customer in the same condition it was in when it arrived at the docks, many more people would eat fish, and the fishing business could greatly expand. He developed an inexpensive container that would keep fish chilled until it got to market. With Birdseye's box, fish arrived in considerably better condition, but it was still not comparable to fresh fish, and a great deal of fish was still lost to spoilage. He knew there had to be a better solution.

Later in life Birdseye developed a pet theory that the subconscious resembled an electronic calculating machine. "If you feed the right information into it," he would say, "it will quietly go to work in mysterious ways of its own and, by-and-by, produce the answer to your problem." He kept thinking about his constant struggle for "fresh food" in Labrador. He remembered the quality of the frozen food, and he believed that was due to its freezing so quickly. How could that be accomplished artificially in climates that were not 40 degrees Fahrenheit below zero? After much reflection following the failure of his container device, Bob said, "my subconscious suddenly told me that perishable foods could be kept perfectly preserved in the same way I had kept them in Labrador—by quick freezing!"

If this could be done industrially, then "fresh" food would be available everywhere at any time of year. The more Bob thought about this, the more he thought this was an idea with huge potential. He left his job and moved to New Jersey, where he persuaded an ice cream company to lend him an area in their plant to conduct experiments in freezing. Eleanor was about to give birth to their third child and second daughter, who would share Eleanor's name. But Bob and Eleanor, after a quiet five years, were off on another adventure.

As with many inventors before him, Bob Birdseye made no scientific discoveries. His inventions were original ideas about how to use existing knowledge—creative thinking. To him, fast freezing was a traditional idea that came from the Inuits, the native inhabitants of Labrador. All his life he credited them. But freezing also has another story.

In human history, the use of fire and heat developed much faster than the harnessing of ice and cold. This may have been because heat, associated with life, is more appealing than cold, which is associated with death. Or it may simply be that it is much easier to learn how to make fire than to make ice. While human beings were relatively quick to heat their food, it took a long time before they learned to chill it, despite the fact that the untapped use of the cold meant that a great deal of food was spoiled and discarded. Spoilage was simply an accepted fact of life. Even in the twentieth century, after commercial freezing was developed, it was a struggle to convince stores that the money they spent on maintaining frozen food was less than the money they lost from spoilage.

For centuries the primary effort to reduce the spoilage

caused by warm temperatures was to bring food to market at night. Animals would be slaughtered at the market to avoid having the meat spoil in transport. Sometimes fish were brought to market live, in ships with tanks.

Frozen food had a sad, almost comical beginning with Sir Francis Bacon, lord chancellor of England, one of the first English scientists, if not the first. He developed theories and questioned their validity, which is the way a scientist works, yet he ended up being perhaps the only martyr to the frozen-food industry.

In March 1626 Bacon was riding in a coach through the Highgate area of North London with the physician of King Charles I. Through his window Bacon gazed at the winter snow still on the ground, which made the landscape look as if it were sprinkled with salt. Though remembered as the great champion of scientific method, Bacon rarely carried out actual experiments. But on this occasion, while speculating with the physician on whether snow could preserve meat the same way that salt did, he suddenly had an urge to try something. Stop the coach!

The two got out and went to a poor woman's house, where they bought a chicken, which she killed and cleaned for them. The men went outside, knelt on the ground, stuffed the bird with snow, and encased it in more snow—exactly the technique used by Bob Birdseye and his Labrador neighbors three centuries later. The cold affected not only the chicken but also Bacon, who became extremely ill. He was taken to a nearby house, where his condition grew worse. He wrote that the experiment of chilling the chicken "succeeded." Only hours after writing the note, Bacon died of pneumonia.

His chicken is often considered the first frozen food, and the reason it is often said that frozen food truly began in 1626.

The year after Bacon's death, Robert Boyle was born in Ireland to the very wealthy earl of Cork, who judged him too sickly for school and so had him taught by tutors at home. A poster child for homeschooling, Boyle became the first true chemist in the modern sense of the word: a researcher who broke the physical world down to basics and tested his theories about their composition through controlled experiments. Unusual for his time, Boyle was interested in understanding everything he could about the phenomenon of coldness. An issue of the day was the question of where cold came from. Heat came from fire, and there were all sorts of theories about the source of fire, but cold was a mystery.

For a long time many Europeans believed cold came from an uncharted island north of the British Isles known as Thule. Aristotle had written that it came from something called *primum frigidum*, but what was this? Aristotle said it was water, which Boyle refuted by showing that material that contained no water, such as metals, could be chilled.

Boyle also pointed out that the surface of water, the part exposed to the air, was the first to freeze. He challenged French philosopher René Descartes's widely held belief that cold was simply the absence of a drifting substance called heat. He also disproved the theory that earth, air, and saltpeter were the source of cold, though he did conduct experiments on how saltpeter and numerous other salts intensified cold.

Bacon before him had had the same idea but couldn't prove it. At the time, producing cold was a trick performed by magicians. Bacon speculated that a number of "magic" stunts that produced cold were done through the use of salts, either common table salt, sodium chloride, or saltpeter, potassium nitrate, to intensify the cold of snow or ice. The use of salts to lower temperature would be a key to the Birdseye freezing process.

Boyle also investigated the nature of ice, showing that it was water in an expanded form. He conducted numerous experiments to show that the volume of ice was greater than the volume of the water from which it was made. Filling the sections of an ice cube tray half full of water and freezing it easily demonstrates this phenomenon: the resulting ice cubes will fill more than half of each section. This is also why, when a bottle of wine freezes, expanding ice forces the cork out of the bottle.

America was to be the place where refrigeration and commercial freezing were developed, leading to rapid advances in the frozen-food industry. This is striking, because Europeans were in the forefront of preserving foods through smoking, salting, and canning. A French chef, Nicolas Appert, invented canning in the time of Napoleon by discovering that food that was heated and hermetically sealed in a jar would not rot. The French and later other Europeans had great enthusiasm for canned or jarred foods and even today feature them prominently in deluxe food shops.

Yet the American embrace of cold as a way to preserve food has also meant that Americans led the way in the manufacturing of refrigerators and freezers. The first refrigerator was a European invention: in 1748 William Cullen, professor of medicine at the University of Glasgow, built a refrigerator based on the fact that evaporating liquids cause a lowering of temperature. Cullen caused a container to lose not only its fluid but its air, becoming a complete vacuum, with the result that the water in a tank that surrounded the refrigerator froze. He wrote a paper on his work and had it published in a local Scottish journal but never attempted to promote the idea.

Nor did all Americans market their ideas. In 1758 Benjamin Franklin wrote a paper on his experiments showing that liquids that evaporate faster than water, such as alcohol, can cause water to freeze. But this did not lead him to build a refrigerator or an ice maker, either of which would have been landmark inventions in 1758.

It was another half century before an American built a refrigerator, but his approach was very different. The device was built in 1802 by a Maryland engineer, Thomas Moore, who, like Birdseye, was less interested in scientific theory than in solving the problem of getting fresh food to market. He built a metal box for butter surrounded by ice in a cedar container tightly insulated with rabbit fur. With this box he was able to carry butter from his farm to the Georgetown market, twenty miles away. Everyone wanted his hard butter rather than the unrefrigerated, coagulated grease of other producers and gladly paid his very high prices. Clearly Moore wanted to start an industry. He patented his box and published a pamphlet about "the newly invented machine called a refrigerator." Industry didn't follow, and Moore earned little money from his invention, but he was hugely influential.

The American dominance in freezers and refrigeration

started with making ice available to everyone, not just the wealthy. In the eighteenth century most European countries stored ice in icehouses, traded it commercially, and used it chiefly to chill drinks. But it was a luxury, sold to the privileged at a very high price. In Russia and France only the royal families were allowed to produce ice.

America started out the same way. The average colonial had no access to summer ice, but icehouses were a feature of the large Virginia slave plantations. George Washington, Thomas Jefferson, and James Madison all had icehouses for enjoying chilled drinks any time of year. In the North, harvesting ice was a low-status, low-wage job; in Philadelphia convicts in prisons were used to make it. Yet wealthy Southerners paid high prices for ice. Further hampering the ice market was the religious belief that using ice out of season was tampering with God's design. There was a similar attitude toward greenhouses.

But America had a revolution with a populist democratic ideology, a belief in the common man, and after that, even while being led by wealthy aristocrats who lived in luxury, the new country often shunned luxury products in favor of popular or inexpensive ones. Icehouses were popularized by a little-remembered but extremely influential man named Frederic Tudor, the son of a distinguished lawyer who had clerked for John Adams. Tudor's father sent three of his sons to Harvard, but not Frederic, who thought it was a waste of time and wanted to move on to making money. He started in a shipping office and, at age seventeen, invented an improved bilge pump for emptying seawater from the hull of a ship.

A few years later he started a business shipping ice to the

Caribbean, particularly Martinique and Cuba. He shipped it carefully insulated in hay but noticed that Caribbeans, understanding nothing of the nature of ice, walked through the streets with it in the midday sun and even attempted to store it in water, which, being warmer, melts the ice. Apparently the idea that water was the source of cold still lingered.

In the 1820s Tudor hired Nathaniel Jarvis Wyeth, another man who had shunned education for commerce. Wyeth revolutionized the ice business, first with a saw-toothed ice cutter that made the blocks more regular and produced them more cheaply, and then with the use of sawdust for insulation. Wyeth produced a series of inventions that by the 1830s made Tudor's the premier icehouse in America. Tudor's ice, much of it cut from Henry David Thoreau's Walden Pond, near Boston, was shipped all over the world.

By the 1830s ice had already transformed the diet of urban Americans. Fresh fruits, vegetables, meat, fish, and milk became increasingly popular. Farmers in upstate New York shipped their milk and other products on ice by train to New York City markets. Fresh fish was brought in on ice from New England. By the Civil War Tudor and his competitors were shipping New England ice to fifty ports and had ships leaving every day. New uses of ice were being contemplated. Couldn't it be used to ship meat? The United States had a surplus of meat, and there was great demand for it in Europe. Tudor became a multimillionaire, and his ice became a common international commodity.

Americans rapidly became the world's greatest consumers of ice, largely because Tudor's and Wyeth's innovations had greatly reduced the cost. Twelve and a half cents could buy one hundred pounds. Southerners became passionate about iced cocktails, the mint julep being one of the most famous. The Port of New Orleans became a major destination for ice, and New Orleans became known for its cocktails. By 1850 New Orleans was buying fifty thousand tons of ice every year, and even though the ice could sell as cheaply as $15 a ton, the volume of sales made ice an important trade. But nowhere was more ice consumed than in New York City, which used twice as much as New Orleans.

By the Civil War, ice in America was used not only for drinks, but also to store food and keep it fresh. Gradually icebox manufacturers understood that the flaw in the Moore model was that there was no circulating air, which helps to cool the ice. That was why, as Boyle had observed, ice froze first on the surface. After 1845 iceboxes had circulating air and were far more effective.

European scientists continued to develop important ideas and avoid their commercial application. In 1834 Charles Saint-Ange Thilorier, a chemist in the School of Pharmacy in Paris, was able to apply enough pressure to carbon dioxide to convert it to a solid carbonic acid. This was an arduous and dangerous undertaking that others had failed at, and Thilorier's assistant had lost both legs in an explosion caused by one of their experiments. He never attempted to commercialize his discovery, although many years later the same carbonic acid, now called dry ice, became an essential part of refrigeration. It is clear that Thilorier understood the potential of his discovery. He mixed dry ice with snow and ether and produced a temperature of −110 degrees Celsius (−166 degrees Fahrenheit), which at the time was by far the coldest temperature ever produced artificially. He simply was not interested in practical applications.

Great progress was made when, in 1859, a Frenchman, Ferdinand Carré, produced a machine that made artificial ice. Though it took some time for this technology to be accepted by industry, eventually it would mean that ice could be made anywhere; it did not have to be cut and stored in the North in winter. But despite this invention, the natural-ice trade prospered for the rest of the century. Maine became the leading exporter, shipping 3,092,400 tons out of state in its best year, 1890.

Some historians fix the date of the first commercial frozen food as 1875, but there may have been earlier attempts. The first US patent for a frozen-fish process was awarded to Enoch Piper of Camden, Maine, in 1862. He froze salmon by placing it on racks under pans of ice and salt, which lowered the air temperature. After the fish was frozen hard, which took about twenty-four hours, he dipped it in water to give it a glassy sheen. More patents followed, and small frozen-fish operations started around coastal New England.

Fish was the usual object of frozen-food experimenting because it was the product that had the greatest losses from spoilage. But it was also the most demanding. People could accept a berry that on thawing had gotten a bit soft and juicy, but it is very hard to sell soft and juicy fish.

In 1875 large-scale operations began freezing food in a room insulated with sawdust, the old Wyeth idea, using ice and salt, an even older idea. Bob saw this type of operation in use for frozen bait in Battle Harbour, Labrador, and described the operation: "In the upper room cracked natural ice and coarse solar [evaporated sea] salt were mixed and filled into rectangular metallic tubes which passed downwardly through the freezing and storage chamber on the ground floor."

Frozen-food production spread from New England to the Great Lakes region to the Pacific Northwest. In 1876 American frozen meat was shipped to England, and by 1881 it was being shipped as far as Australia. By the last decade of the nineteenth century, British Columbia was shipping a million pounds of frozen fish to Europe every year, mostly salmon but also halibut and sturgeon. In 1902 H. A. Baker Sr. was freezing berries in barrels in Puyallup, Washington, and selling them.

But this frozen food had an unenthusiastic public, principally attracted by low prices. Food critics and nutritionists gave it poor ratings, especially the fish. This was an age when prime fish, such as salmon and halibut, were caught in enormous quantities and sold at low prices. But only the fish that had not sold when it was fresh was sold to the freezing companies, so frozen fish started out with very poor quality.

By the 1890s mechanically made ice was increasing frozen-food production. The concept is simple: An object can be chilled by putting it next to something cold. The cold removes warmth from the object next to it, making it also cold. Even before the issue of fast versus slow freezing, there was the issue of direct versus indirect—whether or not the food would have direct contact with the refrigerant, which was usually salt in some form. Direct contact was a problem, since the whole purpose of freezing food was so that it could be conserved without being salted.

Though salt acts by natural laws, it can do so many different and seemingly contradictory things that it appears to operate by magic. A key to understanding salt lies in the common phenomenon of salt melting ice. In many countries more salt by far is used for deicing roads than for any other purpose. In the United States 8 percent of salt production is used for seasoning food and 51 percent for deicing roads.

Anyone who has spent a winter in a place that has ice and snow has seen salt shoveled or spread on roads and sidewalks, with the result that the ice melts. How is it possible that salt melts ice, yet can be used as an agent for freezing? The answer is that salt does not melt ice by raising the temperature but by lowering the freezing point. Water freezes into ice at 32 degrees Fahrenheit, but this is not cold enough to freeze salt. So if water has salt in it, it can be considerably colder than 32 degrees and still be liquid—a liquid as cold as ice.

This can be easily demonstrated with two bowls and a thermometer. Take two identical small bowls, and place five ice cubes in each. In one bowl cover the ice with a quarter cup of table salt. After twenty minutes the unsalted ice won't have melted, but liquid will be forming in the bowl with the salted ice. The salted ice will appear to be melting, but if you measure the temperature of the liquid, it will be 29 degrees, three degrees *below* freezing. After thirty minutes the ice in the other bowl will start to melt. This liquid will be 41 degrees; it will melt because the temperature is above freezing.

Camp Venustus, Birdseye's log cabin in the Bitterroot, in 1910.
Pictured left to right: Willard V. King, Paul Stanton, Clarence Birdseye
wearing his three-piece suit, and Robert Cooley.

Above: Wilfred Grenfell's 1912
sketch poking fun at Birdseye's
hunting skills, found pasted into
Birdseye's diary for October 10, 1912.

Left: A smiling Birdseye in fur
in Labrador, circa 1912.

Clarence and Eleanor's first home, which they had built in Muddy Bay, Labrador.

A stock certificate from May 1923 in Clarence Birdseye's name, for Birdseye Seafoods, his original company in New York.

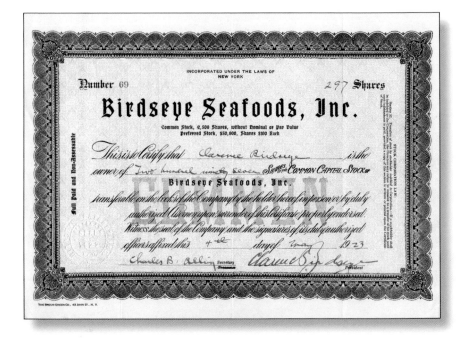

Birdseye with Eleanor and
Henry, the two youngest of
his four children, circa 1929.

Marjorie Merriweather Post, whose
company, General Foods, bought
Birdseye Seafoods in 1929.

An ad for Birdseye Frosted Foods promoting the miraculous quick-freezing process. It ran in the March 2, 1930, issue of the *Springfield Sunday Union and Republican*.

Birdseye in a 1930s home movie, chasing finback whales off of Gloucester Harbor with a tagging harpoon he invented.

Birdseye at work in his office, 1943.

The Birdseye Seafoods building in Gloucester Harbor, circa 1930.

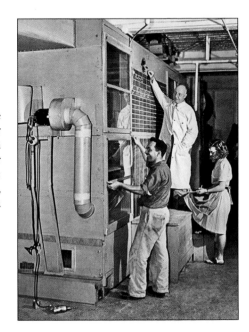

Dehydrating carrots in the laboratory on the second floor of the Birdseye building in Gloucester Harbor in the summer of 1943. Pictured left to right: A. Pothier, Clarence Birdseye, and Helen Josephson Schuster.

The Birdseyes' dining room in their home on Eastern Point, Gloucester, in 1942 or '43. Eleanor is facing the camera; Clarence is opposite her, with his back to the camera. On his left is their elder daughter, Ruth, and on the right their younger son, Henry.

Birdseye in 1947 excitedly serving lobster in his Eastern Point home, which he loved to cook for guests at his "lobster feeds."

Above left: Clarence and Eleanor Birdseye in their home in Peru during the winter of 1954. *Above right:* Birdseye feeding ocelots in Peru.

Birdseye at work in 1955 or '56, upon returning from Peru.

The liquid in the salted bowl will be 21 degrees. So now the salted liquid is eleven degrees below freezing and the melted unsalted ice is nine degrees above freezing. Furthermore, as time goes on, the unsalted melted ice remains at 41 degrees, while in the salted-ice bowl the temperature continues to drop as long as there is some unmelted ice. The salted water drops to 12 degrees, twenty degrees below the freezing point of water, but remains liquid.

Salt does not melt ice—it liquefies it, but the liquid is as cold as ice. It can be carried in coils, it can be sprayed to chill objects, or, as Bob did, it can be pumped inside metal plates, and contact with these plates will cause freezing. Or the brine can be directly applied to food and it will freeze it.

This is important, because a liquid is a much more efficient vehicle for freezing than a solid or a gas. A human without clothes can survive for more than an hour in an air temperature of 35 degrees Fahrenheit without any great difficulty because the cold air is gas. But in water of the same temperature, a liquid, the person will die in minutes. This is also why traditional ice cream makers turn the canister in ice that is liquefied by salt. If you just used solid ice, it would take far longer to freeze the ice cream.

For Bob Birdseye, who was trying to freeze food as quickly as possible in that room in the ice cream factory, a liquid refrigerant was essential. This was why, when he had snow-packed cabbage in barrels in Labrador, he added seawater.

Three hundred years before Bob, Bacon had written about these ideas, though he clearly did not completely understand them. But he was right. In the twentieth century, with more science available, using salt became the standard method of freezing.

The first industrial freezer in the United States was the Ottoson brine freezer. Food was submerged in a brine solution at freezing point. The brine had the same percentage of salt as the cellular composition of the food, which was supposed to keep the salt from being absorbed by the food. But this equilibrium was nearly impossible to maintain, and often the food became unbearably salty.

In 1921 Paul W. Peterson built the first "indirect freezer"—a machine in which the refrigerant and the food never come into contact. The food was packed in containers and immersed in a liquid refrigerant. In 1923, the year Bob started his first frozen-food company, Gordon F. Taylor developed a new kind of direct-contact freezer in which a whole fish moved on a conveyor belt under a spray of cold water and then was frozen with brine. The frozen fish was then sprayed with water again to wash off the brine and give it a crystalline glaze of ice. From Bob's point of view, the interesting idea in Taylor's machine was the use of a conveyor belt for mass production.

By the 1920s, when Bob started thinking about commercially freezing food, fast freezing was well known in science, and even industry had experimented with it. The earliest commercial fast-frozen food, which was whole fish in salt and ice, had been produced in 1915 while Bob was in Labrador and not noticing. Also by the 1920s European scientists had expounded on fast freezing and the principals of crystallization, but in reality most frozen food was still slow frozen and made from the cheapest, poorest-quality fresh food. State laws tried to protect consumers from the terrible frozen food. In the state of New York slow-frozen food could not be sold unless a store posted a sign over its entrance in letters a minimum of eight inches tall stating FROZEN FOOD SOLD HERE. New York State also banned the serving of frozen food in its prisons.

Perhaps Birdseye didn't arrive at the idea of freezing sooner because of how bad frozen food's reputation was. At the 1883 International Fisheries Exhibition, a highly influential gathering in London of all the North Atlantic fishing nations, which influenced attitudes about everything from eating fish to managing fisheries, frozen fish had been presented and received horrible reviews. The press described its smell as a "stink" and its look as "withered." Forty years later this was still the prevailing image of frozen food.

There was a minor breakthrough in its acceptance during World War I, when the US Army bought small quantities of frozen fish and chicken to feed soldiers. This led to a considerable amount of talk about frozen food after the war, though few people actually ate it.

By the time Bob began his experiments with freezing food in 1923, frozen food had been around for fifty years, and all the technology he needed for the kind of production he envisioned was available. But, by his own confession, he knew almost nothing of it. He did not know about Ottoson's machine, or Peterson's, or most of the studies and debates. He knew only what he had learned about freezing in Labrador. But this had taught him something no one else seemed to understand: he could piece together the techniques that other people had developed and make a product that would be astoundingly good. This was his belief, and it didn't matter that when he told people he would make frozen fish "as good as fresh," almost everyone would scrunch up their nose or roll their eyes.

In 1923 Bob set out to start his own frozen-fish company, Birdseye Seafood, in New York City by selling $20,000 in stock. He looked everywhere for investors in his big idea. Henry Ford had expressed interest in frozen food, so Birdseye made an effort to get his backing, but he got no response. Then the Clothel Refrigerating Company, which produced refrigerators for the navy, became interested in Bob's venture and provided him a space on White Street, a short distance from the Fulton Street Market, where wholesale fresh fish was bought and sold.

What was new about Bob's work was as much in the packaging as in the preparation of food. He was still primarily interested in figuring out how to get the product from wholesaler to retailer to consumer in a sanitary, efficient, convenient package. If his boxes had worked better, he might not have gone into freezing.

Perhaps the most famous Birdseye myth is that Bob went to a store, spent $7 on salt, ice, and an electric fan, and with these reproduced the Labrador winter and froze a fish. There is an element of truth to this, which is that this was how Bob worked: he found a few banal household items and solved a problem.

The problem with frozen food was not only that it didn't

freeze quickly enough but also that it wasn't cold enough. Birdseye estimated that a piece of meat was not truly frozen until it reached –96 degrees Fahrenheit. Existing commercial freezing was done at about 25 degrees, only a few degrees below the freezing point.

Bob always chose low technology over high, and so in his home in Yorktown Heights, in New York's Westchester County, he experimented with various salts and even dry ice. His salts had to drop the temperature very low and very quickly. Years later Bob would recall, "Production of perishable foods, dressed at the point of production and quick frozen in consumer packages, was initiated, so far as I am aware, in the kitchen of my own home late in 1923 when I experimentally packaged rabbit meat and fish fillets in candy boxes and froze the packages with dry ice."

He discovered that all that was necessary for quick freezing was that the temperature pass very quickly out of the first freezing temperature, which is from 33 degrees to 23 degrees Fahrenheit. He eventually settled on calcium chloride in a solution he could maintain at –45 degrees, which was the temperature of some of the coldest days in Labrador. Below that point, crystallization is rapid and crystals become very small. To speed up freezing, he had to freeze smaller amounts. Freezing at the time was an entirely wholesale business, and huge blocks of food, including whole sides of beef, were frozen. Fruits were frozen into blocks of as much as four hundred pounds. The food was placed in a barely freezing environment and frozen over a number of days. Not only were these quantities too massive to be frozen quickly, they also had no retail market, because what could a family do with a frozen side of beef or four hundred pounds of strawberries?

He developed his own machine for packing and freezing fish fillets. The machine weighed twenty tons, considerably larger and heavier than Clothel's two-ton refrigerator. In 1924 Bob was awarded his first patent for this fish-freezing process. In his patent application dated April 18, 1924, he made the following claim: "It is well known that fish like many other dietary articles has been frozen for the purpose of suspending, or preventing, decomposition through oxidation, bacteriological or other action, but the present invention goes much further than that and accomplishes results heretofore unknown in the seafood industry."

If Bob didn't pioneer actual freezing, he had to pioneer most everything else in his process. He experimented with the different heat-insulating properties of fiberboard, cardboard, cork, and wood. His ideas were so new that the National Bureau of Standards could not furnish him with any information on the insulating properties of fiberboard. No one had tested it, so he did. His first patent makes clear that his concern was as much with packaging as with freezing itself. The patent goes into elaborate diagrams and explanation of the packaging—insulated fiberboard boxes—and was the first of many patents Birdseye was awarded for packaging.

One of Bob's first true innovations was packing fish in corrugated cardboard, fiberboard, and eventually waxed cardboard, rather than the traditional balsa wood boxes used for salted fish. Balsa wood worked well enough, but his quality frozen fish was going to cost more than people were accustomed to paying for frozen food. He wanted to produce it as inexpensively as he could without sacrificing quality. The wooden boxes cost $1 for every pound they held. They were supposed to be returnable, but customers seldom bothered. Later in 1924 Bob patented his second, improved box. He was very concerned with eliminating all air pockets within the package of fish, because bacteria, which led to decomposition and illness, could grow in these spaces.

Bob, like Gordon Taylor with his conveyor-belt freezer, froze one fish at a time. Whole fish went through the extra steps of being skinned and filleted. The fillet not only froze faster but was easier to thaw and use. His quick-frozen fish went on the market in 1924. Birdseye Seafood was broke within a year. New Yorkers didn't want to eat frozen food. What had gone wrong? Was it his idea? As Bob later in life would tell young people, the key to success is not just having an idea and believing in it, but being willing to gamble. What had gone wrong with his seafood company was not the idea or that he'd been overly ambitious. It was just the opposite. He had not thought big enough. If he wanted to sell frozen food in a world where people didn't eat frozen food or even have freezers, he had to create more than a company; he had to create a whole new industry. This was a gigantic undertaking. But he believed he was on the path to an important innovation. He had solved a few of the problems, but he needed more time and more money to solve the others.

Though they had three small children to raise, Bob and Eleanor gambled everything on this big idea to make it work and sold their life insurance policy of $2,500 or, according to some, $2,250. The gamble was a testament to Eleanor's faith in Bob throughout their marriage. She also used to explain to their children, "Dad was born ahead of his time. There is so much going on in his head, the world can't even catch up." Their daughter-in-law, Kellogg's wife, Gypsy, said of her, "I call her Saint Eleanor. He was just the most fortunate man to have had her for a wife."

Bob and Eleanor sold their house in Westchester and, with their three children and a fourth expected, moved to Gloucester, Massachusetts, the oldest fishing town in the United States, to start anew.

CHAPTER SEVEN

A Very Big Deal

When the Birdseyes arrived in Gloucester, the city had just celebrated its three hundredth birthday. Founded in 1623 as an English fishing station, it remained, and still is today, one of the leading fishing ports of the United States. Its deep and extensive harbor, on the headlands of a peninsula but in the sheltered lee of the wind, makes it the ideal port for New England's richest fishing grounds.

In 1873 the population had grown to 15,397, making it the most populous town in Massachusetts, and so a new charter designated that it was now a city. When the Birdseyes arrived, in the mid-1920s, most of the population directly or indirectly made their living from the fishery. In addition to the fishermen and their families, there were the "lumpers," or dockworkers, and the ancillary trades that repaired ships, made iron fittings, and manufactured oilskins for the fisherman to wear. Glue was made from fish skins and, in the 1880s, sold worldwide by William LePage.

The people in Gloucester lived a hard and tradition-bound life. A close-knit community of skilled blue-collar workers was an ideal place for starting a new industry. It was a hardworking town with a tough waterfront of bars and merchants. The harbor was crammed with the masts and canvas sails of some 150 fishing schooners, as well as fat-hulled square-rigged barks that arrived with sea salt from Trapani, Sicily. The Gloucester fish industry used enormous quantities of salt—one of the things Bob was about to change.

At the time, there was already an inventor in town, John Hays Hammond Jr., the brother of Bob's former backer in the fur trade, Harris Hammond. Only two years younger than Bob, John was known for inventing the remote control. He also came up with a radio-controlled gyroscope system that allowed him to pilot an unmanned yacht on a 120-mile round-trip between Gloucester harbor and Boston in 1914. Fishermen encountering the ghost ship at sea were disconcerted.

During World War I Hammond invented a system to protect the remote control from enemy interference and then an electronic guidance system for targeting warheads. In addition, he worked on the first radio-guided torpedo and invented, among other things, an eye wash, a harmonic organ, an altitude-measuring system for airplanes, a magnetic bottle cap remover, and a meat baster.

Like other eager young inventors of the time, Hammond was constantly coming up with ideas for whatever problems confronted him. By the end of his life, his more than four hundred patents would outdo even Birdseye by about a hundred patents. Perhaps most telling of the disparity between their lives was that when Bob and Eleanor were settling in Gloucester, Hammond was building a castle on the west side of the harbor.

By the summer of 1925 the Birdseyes were living in a comfortable house with a wide porch at 1 Beach Road, near an exclusive golf club. It was not a particularly deluxe neighborhood, but the neighborhoods away from the harbor were considered somewhat better, because they were away from the harbor's smell. The house was an easy walk to what is known as the backshore, the part of Gloucester that is on the open Atlantic, with rough and majestic granite boulders and long sand beaches.

Bob loved the historic industrial fishing port and spent more years in Gloucester than in any other place in his life. The city itself is a confusing series of inlets, coves, and peninsulas, but to find the town center, one had only to sniff. The final stop on the Cape Ann peninsula after the picturesque Manchester-by-the-Sea was often called Gloucester-by-the-Smell. Lining most of Gloucester harbor, which includes the downtown, were fish flakes (rough-hewn wooden drying racks for salt cod), many of them owned by the Gorton-Pew Fisheries, a merger of the city's two largest seafood companies. Salt cod was Gloucester's biggest product, and it had to spend weeks drying in the sun—and giving off a rich, fishy odor. For people who grew up in Gloucester it was just the smell of home, but it made a strong impression on visitors.

● ● ●

With his infectious enthusiasm Birdseye was able to secure investors for a new venture, the General Seafoods Corporation. He brought in Wall Streeter Wetmore Hodges, and Hodges brought in two colleagues from J. P. Morgan, Isaac L. Rice and Bassett Jones. Together the three invested $375,000, which had the spending power of almost $5 million in today's economy.

Though Hodges was a young man, bringing him in was an important step. He knew many powerful New York financial people, and his father was Charles Hodges, a vice president of the American Radiator Company. Bob managed to interest the company in the future manufacturing of freezer units and was beginning to lay the foundations of the frozen-food industry. His new company was small, but he had numerous investors and backers interested in taking a chance on his ideas. Bob made his brother Kellogg a vice president of General Seafoods, and Kellogg moved to Gloucester with his wife, May, who was from Massachusetts, and their two children.

In 1926 Birdseye bought a building on a peninsula in the downtown harborfront area known as the Fort, one of the oldest neighborhoods in Gloucester. The first floor was used to develop frozen-food experiments, the second-floor offices for developing and planning the company's future.

Despite the modest size of the building, Bob's ambitions for General Seafoods were large. He chose that name because he imagined his company would have the esteem in the fish industry that General Electric and General Motors did in energy and transportation.

In fact, it was never his plan to just sell frozen fish. Most of the top people he hired were either financiers or engineers. His goal was to develop a frozen-food process, design new machinery, patent his ideas, and then either license them to other companies or sell his own company. Most important were the patents for equipment that could enable a large company that had the money to make frozen food a national or even international industry. The new company, Birdseye imagined, could go far beyond seafood and be called General Foods. In 1960 Joe Guinane, Bob's first manager and an engineer who worked on the design of new machinery, remarked that "there was not a frozen-food item that I do not recall Birdseye experimenting with at one time or another in the early days. He tried all kinds of things—not only seafood, meats, and vegetables, but baked and unbaked goods, as well as cooked foods." Birdseye envisioned the entire future of frozen food.

General Seafoods first produced thousands of pounds of haddock fillets frozen in rectangular cardboard boxes. Bob, who had once wanted to taste every food possible, now wanted to freeze any edible cuisine, an obsession that would stay with him the rest of his life. He prowled the docks for anything unusual that he could try freezing and let the Gloucester dragger captains know of his peculiar interest. Because of that, Birdseye froze whale, shark, porpoise, and, according to one account, an alligator.

Birdseye's inquisitiveness also led him to examine packaging and many other devices, in addition to freezing machinery. His colleague J. J. Barry developed an electronic machine for trimming fish. Birdseye invented a new brining and fish-scaling machine, which would dramatically cut manual labor. Although other electronic fish scalers existed, those would stall out when hitting a fin; Birdseye's did not. It was able to pick up fillets, wash them, and then brine them.

Bob was so excited about his machine that in July 1925 he wrote to Rice that it filleted 23½ haddock per minute, and he was anticipating a newer, better motor that might do as many as 50 per minute. Filleting machines would become the big thing of the 1920s seafood business, and by the 1930s both fresh and frozen fillets would dominate the seafood market. Filleting operations from the Boston Fish Pier and Nova Scotia came to Gloucester to look at Bob's work. The men from Boston told him that in the next twelve months they planned to produce and sell ten million pounds of haddock fillets.

The real game changer was Birdseye's freezing process. Of his more than two hundred inventions, the most important was one he applied for a patent for on June 18, 1927: patent 1,773,079, which began the frozen-food industry. Bob begins the application by asserting:

> *My invention relates to methods of treating food products by refrigerating the same, preferably by "quick" freezing the product into a frozen block, in which the pristine qualities and flavors of the product are retained for a substantial period after the block has been thawed.*

His invention description included every step of the process, including how to pack fish fillets in a box. Among the advantages he claimed for his method was that it was "indirect"—the product had no contact with the refrigerant—and that the frozen food came out in a package suitable for marketing to the consumer. He then claimed to have invented, for the first time ever, a way of producing frozen food "as a practical, commercial article of commerce."

He accomplished the quick-freeze process by eliminating air and packing food very tightly into cartons holding a two-inch-thick block, then pressing those cartons between two plates that were kept between –20 and –50 degrees Fahrenheit. The carton was held between the freezing plates for seventy-five minutes. The blocks not only froze the food solid but compacted it into a tight, regular rectangle, assuring complete freezing in a short period of time and no spaces for bacteria to enter.

Without making a scientific breakthrough, Bob had developed a process for freezing food on which an entirely new industry was founded. It was called multiplate freezing. His basic commercial freezing system remained the standard in the industry for decades to come, and in 1946 the *New Yorker* magazine stated that the only change in freezing since Birdseye's invention was that the plates were now hollow. Hollowing the plates and putting an ammonia-based refrigerant inside was, in fact, only one of Bob's improvements after the initial invention was created.

However, the breakthrough did not immediately clear the way of obstacles for General Seafoods to become the General Motors of food. In the world of inventing, inventers were often too far ahead of their time. They produced cars before there were paved roads or constructed telephones before there was telephone wiring. The classic example was

Thomas Edison, who developed a lightbulb that would have been commercially viable if only there had been an electric grid to hook it up to. Birdseye's problem was that the necessary infrastructure had not yet been built.

Bob first faced the issue in the summer of 1927, when he froze 1,666,033 pounds of seafood and wanted to ship it to the Midwest, where consumers had no fresh seafood. At the time there were no trucks or train cars capable of transporting frozen food, and no warehouses cold enough to ship the food to. Birdseye's company lacked the distribution network necessary for frozen foods. In addition, retail stores did not have equipment cold enough for holding or displaying top-quality quick-frozen food.

Then, too, there was the daunting problem of getting the consumer to accept the product. People laughed at the idea of frozen food. Most people thought that if meat was frozen, it was a whole side or the entire body of an animal. Frozen vegetables were unheard of, and the only frozen fruit people knew of was strawberries, most of which were purchased industrially for making ice cream or jam and jelly. Fish in fillets was still a new idea. They placed white notices inside each box of fish that stated, in red lettering, THE PRODUCT IN THIS CONTAINER IS FROZEN HARD AS MARBLE BY A MARVELOUS NEW PROCESS WHICH SEALS IN EVERY BIT OF JUST-FROM-THE-OCEAN FLAVOR.

To complicate matters, Birdseye had also drifted into the middle of a major debate of his time about whether industry was destroying the livelihoods of artisans and craftsmen. Labor unions that represented butchers, seafood processors, and poultry workers came out early and emphatically against frozen food. They believed that if this new idea caught on, food would all be processed in frozen-food factories and their workers would be out of business. At the time, Bob denied this. Sadly, they were right, although frozen food has not hurt them nearly as much as supermarket chains, which in turn are now being threatened by online food-delivery services. The canning industry also feared frozen food, and after Bob established the idea that frozen food would come in cartons rather than cans, can makers turned against him as well.

New ideas generate a great deal of distrust. Railroads were unenthusiastic about getting into the transport of frozen food, because they imagined huge liability for shipments that accidentally thawed. Public health officials and even some scientists at the US Department of Agriculture, where Birdseye believed he had friends, opposed frozen foods. The scientific community reasoned that if fast freezing preserved everything in its natural state, then pests and diseases would be preserved in the freezing process as well and contaminate food that would be shipped around the country. Bob bitterly complained that every time he launched a new product, he was forced to spend a great deal of research-and-development money at the Massachusetts Institute of Technology proving that it was safe to eat. He had to prove that his freezing process killed trichinae (which cause trichinosis) in pork and corn borers in corn before he could get approval to sell those foods as frozen products. Vegetables in particular were held in high suspicion by health authorities, because unlike the heating process in canning, freezing offers no sterilization.

• • •

In spite of public opinion, Birdseye solved most of the problems that he had pondered for multiple freezing. Now he could quickly produce a large amount of frozen food with indirect freezing, a limited air space, and a final boxed product in a convenient form suitable for marketing to home consumers.

His packaging invention came ten years before plastic was invented, when there wasn't another readily available strong, waterproof wrapping material. Wax paper gave little protection from moisture and completely deteriorated during thawing. Vegetable parchment wasn't waterproof and stuck to the box. The company had to get creative. They were able to coat the parchment with paraffin, which kept it from sticking while thawing, but that dried out in the freezer. They bought cellophane from France, but that disintegrated when it came into contact with wet fish. Exasperated, they persuaded the DuPont Company, which made cellophane, to add a waterproof coating to its product. The French chemical company saw the commercial potential and went into production, even though, at the start, General Seafoods of Gloucester was its only customer for it. New kinds of ink and glue also had to be developed, because frozen-food cartons became soggy as soon as they began thawing.

Bob was still focused on his central task of changing the freezing process. He developed an improved freezing machine: the continuous-belt freezer. Instead of plates, this machine had two two-inch-thick metal belts; a calcium chloride spray at −45 degrees Fahrenheit chilled the belts, which were adjusted so the packages would be pressed between them, freezing them from the bottom and the top so that the product in the box froze quickly. This was intended not only for greater production but for a future freezing all kinds of foods in different-sized boxes. The space between the belts was adjustable so packages would always fit tightly.

It was at first difficult to find the right belts. Birdseye started with Swedish belts made of watch-spring steel. He then tried copper, bronze, and Monel, a corrosion-resistant nickel alloy. The solution was stainless steel, a steel alloy with chromium to resist corrosion. Stainless steel had been in development for more than a decade but was not widely available until the 1930s. When Birdseye first explained the machine to investor Isaac Rice, Rice called it a "Goldberg contraption." Rube Goldberg was an engineer famous for cartoons in which he invented absurdly complicated machines to accomplish simple tasks.

Bob had built a contraption with a future, an improvement on multiplate freezing that was good enough to be the basis of a new industry. The drawback, the Goldberg aspect, was that his machine was fifty yards long, weighed twenty tons, and could be operated only in a cold, insulated room. The company bought a neighboring building in 1928 to house the huge machine.

Yet for all this innovation, General Seafoods still lacked a suitable transportation system and warehouses. Even if the company did manage to get its frozen food to retail stores, the stores had no way of keeping the food frozen. As a result, General Seafoods sometimes sold directly to large families, and stores that bought the frozen food often thawed it out to sell as fresh food. In 1928 the first retail-store freezer became available and, according to Bob, it cost as much as the entire rest of the store.

All these new ideas out at the Fort in Gloucester were not happening in a vacuum. Great innovations often feed off other visions, eventually creating a critical mass of thought that makes something happen. While the Birdseye group was struggling to invent a new food industry, so were many other companies. It was the dawn of many emerging food industries, which were putting new foods on the market and packaging them in new ways. In 1928, the year of the new freezer, both the slicing machine and bubble gum were invented. The following year 7UP soda debuted and Harland Sanders opened his first fried chicken restaurant in a gas station in Corbin, Kentucky.

The year the commercial freezer was invented, Kraft put Velveeta cheese on the market. Before 1928 cheese was sold from a wheel or block under unrefrigerated glass domes, and slices were cut as needed. Exposure caused the cut end to dry up, discolor, and crack, so retailers had to cut the dried end off every time they served a new customer, wasting a large part of the block. If better refrigeration and a good airtight wrapper like the one Birdseye worked on had been available, processed cheese might never have been invented. Chicago cheese merchant James Lewis Kraft began experimenting with a cheese-based factory blend. He made a fortune selling canned processed cheese to the army during World War I and continued developing the product and the company after the war was over. In part he combated spoilage by packaging cheese in small amounts. Velveeta, wrapped in tinfoil and packed in individual wooden boxes, was his crowning achievement: it melted so smoothly, it seemed like velvet. Kraft was not originally trying to make cheese melt well, but the "meltiness" of his processed cheese changed the way Americans ate and became a staple of the American diet, used in macaroni and cheese, cheeseburgers, grilled cheese sandwiches, and au gratin everything.

And Birdseye and Kraft were not the only innovators of food packaging at the time. In 1929 milk was first sold in cartons, and a British scientist, E. A. Murphy, whipped latex rubber with a kitchen mixer and created foam rubber.

By 1928 most of General Seafoods' impressive production of frozen food had not been sold, unlike Velveeta. Birdseye and his coworkers were learning to freeze meats, fruits, and vegetables, yet they could not develop the market. Advertising and marketing cost money, which the Birdseye company did not have enough of. Bob had an idea for an improved freezer but didn't have the money to develop it. The bottom line was that General Seafoods needed more capital; without that money it could never grow into a major industry.

Banks would not finance the new frozen-food industry. They would finance the old bulk freezing operations, but this new packaged frozen-food business seemed too risky. Birdseye once remarked that "a bank would no more loan on our inventory than on ice stacked in Death Valley!" Therefore, Birdseye had to seek another investor.

• • •

Eventually, Clarence Birdseye found someone interested in the future of frozen foods, and her name was Marjorie Merriweather Post. She was the daughter and heiress of Charles William Post, who had made a fortune in Battle Creek, Michigan, building the Postum Cereal Company. When she died, in 1973, her estimated wealth was $200 million—more than $1 billion today.

According to Birdseye legend, while Post was vacationing on her yacht in 1926, she sailed into Gloucester harbor. Her cook went into town for provisions and that night served her a goose. She was shocked to learn that this delicious goose, so tender, so—well, fresh-tasting—had been frozen. Who froze this goose? How did they do it? She wanted to know. Supposedly Marjorie, in her elegant dress, went down to the fishy, rough-and-tumble Fort and toured the General Seafoods plant. She then spent the next three years trying to persuade her husband or, in some versions of the story, her father to buy the Birdseye company. Eventually Postum secured the company for a record $22 million. The fabled story has been told in most Birdseye accounts and in obituaries for Marjorie Post that appeared in both the *Washington Post* and the *New York Times*. Yet there is little concrete evidence, and problematic parts of the story make its truth questionable.

Regardless, it is a fact that Marjorie sailed into Gloucester around 1926, as there is a photograph of her huge four-masted bark in the harbor.

The story overlooked what an accomplished woman Post was in her own right. She definitely did not go to her father. He died in 1914 and left her in charge of the company, which, as principal shareholder, she ran successfully for eight years.

Edward Francis Hutton, the second of her four husbands, an aggressive financial tycoon who had founded the E. F. Hutton brokerage house before the marriage, took over the company in 1922. Marjorie, who had been trained by her father, worked with her husband, and together they acquired a dozen food companies. They rarely disagreed, at least publicly. The goose story described Marjorie Post as a self-indulgent heiress who, because she enjoyed her dinner, was prepared to spend millions on a whim—unless a male figure reined her in. But the truth was completely different.

Marjorie Post's father, Charles Post, was born in Springfield, Illinois. He had a high-strung, restless nature and was given to depression, but he had a history of starting up new enterprises from ideas that excited him. Like Bob Birdseye, once successful, he was eager to move on to the next idea. In 1890 he traveled with his wife and three-year-old Marjorie to Michigan, where he checked into the Battle Creek Sanitarium, under the direction of Dr. John Harvey Kellogg, famous for a treatment of "inspirational talks" and a grain-based vegetarian diet. Kellogg and his brother, Will K. Kellogg, had concocted a line of health foods for their sanitarium, including "caramel coffee," a caffeine-free hot drink made from bread crusts, bran, and molasses. Charles emerged weak and emaciated—he restored his health with the Christian Scientists, who included a little meat in his diet—but he had gleaned a lot from his experience.

Post was so taken with Dr. Kellogg's operation that in 1892 he opened his own sanitarium, on a ten-acre farm outside Battle Creek, and called it La Vita Inn. He was clearly imitating Kellogg, with a similar treatment and a special diet, even including his own version of a caramel coffee that was also made with molasses and bran, as well as wheat berries. In 1894 he published a book, *I Am Well*, which promoted "mind-cure," a trendy idea among new American business-men that illness was not real and the human mind could cure all. Dr. Kellogg had been successful with several books on his health and diet ideas.

Neither Post's book nor his inn caught on. But he had an idea that he might be able to sell his coffee substitute. He started with mail order and in 1895 began selling it to gro-cers, branding the beverage Postum.

The first year Post lost $800 on Postum. That was when he realized that his real talent was writing advertising copy. He launched a national advertising campaign that offered to save people from the evils of coffee, which he claimed caused heart attacks, laziness, blindness, cowardice, and stupidity. Does coffee, he asked, "neutralize all of your ef-forts to make money and fame?" Soon Post was becoming wealthy from Postum sales. In 1897 he came out with a ce-real called Grape-Nuts. In the baking process, this concoc-tion of whole wheat, yeast, and malted barley flour turned starch into dextrose, the sugar found in grapes, and so the nuggets were "grape nuts." Always an aggressive and inven-tive copywriter, Post claimed that his products sent people "on the road to Wellville." Combined earnings from Postum and Grape-Nuts were more than $1 million in 1903. By the time Post died, eleven years later, he was one of the five larg-est advertisers in the country, with an annual ad budget of $1 million. Post eventually lost interest in most of the company's operations but had continued to insist on writing all the advertising copy himself.

The Kelloggs followed Post's example. Will, the underpaid, mistreated kid brother with no medical degree, had the job of boiling wheat dough and pressing it into thin sheets through rollers. One morning in 1894 the dough was too dry and flaked off as it came out of the rollers. From that he developed a process called tempering, which produced flakes, and the concept of cereal flakes was born. He began experimenting with other grains. Corn was particularly popular. Will wanted to do what Post had done, but his brother was a man of science who felt that selling cereal would be beneath him. Finally, in 1906, Will broke away from his brother and formed his own cereal company, which, like Post's, distinguished itself by its large and successful advertising campaigns.

Kellogg and Post were the beginning of modern marketing, paving the way for businessmen who liked to be in touch with all areas of their companies. While Kellogg stuck close to his original cereal products, Post wanted a huge company with many new food products and ideas, as he believed that any good idea would sell to the public if the right advertising campaign were supplied. By acquiring small, promising food companies, Marjorie Post made the company much bigger, and with her husband's connections it grew into a food giant. In 1925 Post bought Jell-O, an ambitious company that had expanded the market in flavored gelatin through advertising innovations, such as distributing Jell-O recipe books. In 1926 Post bought Baker's chocolate, which was one of America's oldest and biggest chocolate companies, and in 1928 it bought Maxwell House coffee. The Post company, with its skill, funding for marketing, and taste for new food ideas, was the perfect investor for Birdseye's General Seafoods.

In considering the acquisition of the Gloucester-based food company, Marjorie Merriweather Post would have done more than just visit the plant; she would have found out everything she could about Birdseye's business and ideas and the value of the company and its patents. Marjorie would have considered the potential for marketing and advertising. She would have talked it over with her husband, not to get permission but because he had financial expertise. And together they would have gone to Wall Street to raise the money for the deal.

Bob's company was of obvious appeal to the Postum Cereal Company. General Seafoods had developed the ideas and technology for an entirely new food industry, but it lacked capital and had a huge image problem that would require skilled marketing and advertising. Each company had what the other lacked. In addition, Bob always said that he and his partners had been trying to sell the company for some time, partly because they did not have the capital to develop their ideas and partly because the original plan had always been to make money by selling the company. Wetmore Hodges decided to go to people he knew at the Wall Street investment firm Goldman Sachs.

Bob always liked to call the deal to buy out his company the most money ever paid for a patent—an impressive victory, considering the fact that most of the important patents had not yet been granted and wouldn't come through until 1930. The total $23.5 million price was for the names, patents, patent applications, and all assets, but Postum actually bought all the patents for $20 million and the rest of the company for the remainder. Birdseye's personal share was about $1 million.

The acquisition was announced on May 7, 1929, with Postum as the majority owner. On July 27 its stockholders approved the purchase. Post's company reorganized as General Foods, going on the New York Stock Exchange on July 25 for the first time under its new name. It liked the Birdseye name (preserving it in the title of General Foods' new Birds Eye Frosted Food Division) as well as the Birdseye idea of becoming the leading food company.

For Clarence Birdseye, the timing was remarkable, as the deal would have been canceled had negotiations continued a few months longer. On October 29, 1929, known as Black Tuesday, the stock market took the greatest fall in history, and companies disappeared, along with millions of jobs and many people's fortunes. The Great Depression, an economic crisis that continued for ten years, had begun. In that climate it is unlikely that $23 million would have been spent to start a new industry, but the deal had already been made.

CHAPTER EIGHT

Magic

While millions of people began the 1930s in financial ruin, Birdseye went into the Depression with an extra $1 million, the equivalent of more than $13 million today. Taxes at the time were low, and a man with $1 million was very rich. Bob and his family were able to live comfortably during the worst years of the Depression, and he continued his frozen-food experiments with a good salary as the director of research for General Foods' new Gloucester-based frozen-food division, since the Birdseye mind was part of the deal.

Bob had a few ideas about how to spend his windfall, but he did not have the eccentricity of a Hammond to build himself a medieval castle. To him a baronial mansion seemed more appropriate. He had his seventeen-room mansion built in the Eastern Point peninsula on the tip of Gloucester harbor, in an astounding seven months, between December 1930 and the end of June 1931. When completed, it was valued at $200,000 ($3 million today), an impressive expenditure for the Depression.

Birdseye imported delicate floral wallpaper from France for the dining room. There was a screened porch, a pine-paneled study, a sunporch with a wall fountain. The five spacious bedrooms upstairs afforded stunning views of Gloucester harbor and out to the open bay and the Atlantic. Artwork wasn't of interest—notable since in Gloucester many people collected the excellent locally produced art in that period, as they do today. There was a shooting range in the basement, though Bob ended up using the basement more as a laboratory for his experiments.

The Birdseyes did not have a trendsetting style. The closest the house came to it was, not surprisingly, the kitchen. Stainless steel was a new idea that rarely made it into home kitchens. Don Wonson, who grew up next door to the Birdseyes, recalled that "the kitchen was all stainless steel. He was very meticulous about the kitchen, wiping it down with towels—stainless-steel sinks, big refrigerators, big stainless-steel with double doors. A big freezer in the kitchen. More refrigerators downstairs. Stainless-steel counters, even the drain boards were stainless steel."

Bob handpicked every detail. In an age when there were no blacktop driveways, he put in an innovative tar-and-crushed-granite pavement. The garage, which housed the Birdseyes' three cars, was very large, with a spacious apartment on the top floor. The huge wooden garage doors with massive iron strap hinges resembled gates to a castle.

For people who were known for their simplicity and

straightforwardness, it was an imposing mansion on a hill. Four tall white pillars announced the front entrance. Bob named the house Wyndiecote and finally had a home worthy of the name. It resembled the grand bourgeois look of his first home in Cobble Hill, Brooklyn, yet Bob was almost always seen in his little Ford.

What was Bob to do now that he had achieved his goal? His manager, Joe Guinane, said, "He was an impatient man and had little interest in the routine affairs involved in running the business. Once the problem was solved, he was eager to turn to something new." Some suggested that he retire. After all, he was in his mid-forties and had made his fortune. But Bob just said, "Following one's curiosity is much more fun than taking things easy."

He was not yet through with frozen food. After all, it's one thing to conceive of an idea and build the equipment to make it, but it is a very different problem to make the idea take hold in society. Frozen food was still a long way from being a real industry and an accepted part of American shopping and eating. All he had accomplished was getting the right people and money behind the project.

Bob continued his work, only now as an executive for the Birds Eye Frosted Food Division. One of the early marketing decisions, along with changing Birdseye to Birds Eye, was calling the food "frosted food" to emphasize that it was something completely different from the frozen food that people knew.

Bob later wrote, "Quick freezing was conceived, born, and nourished on a strange combination of ingenuity, stickto-itiveness, sweat, and good luck." By the fall of 1929 the new Birds Eye division was operating at capacity, stockpiling frozen food for its launch. On March 6, 1930, the Springfield, Massachusetts, newspaper ran an advertisement with the headline "The Most Revolutionary Idea in the History of Food Will Be Revealed in Springfield Today."

The vaunted marketing and advertising experts of the former Postum Cereal Company had chosen Springfield as their site for launching twenty-seven frozen items, including porterhouse steaks, spring lamb chops, sliced ham, pork sausages, June peas, spinach, Oregon cherries, loganberries, red raspberries, fillets of haddock and sole, and bluepoint oysters. Twelve "demonstrators" were sent to ten participating stores. The demonstrators—all of whom were women, as were most of the shoppers—and the store employees had undergone a three-day training program, largely focused on how to explain the difference between slow and fast freezing. Each store was given a display freezer worth $1,500, which was far more expensive than most of these small family stores could have afforded. The frozen foods were sold on consignment.

The freezers were far from flawless, however, and a team of mechanics assigned to the ten stores was constantly checking temperatures and making repairs and adjustments, because it would have made a calamitous first impression if any of the food was less than top quality.

The owners of those first stores were people who believed that frozen food was the future and were willing to proselytize to a wary public. Paul G. Seyler, who worked for Thrift Stores in Springfield, one of the first self-service chains, said, "I clearly recall that it took five minutes of fast talking to sell a reluctant housewife a thirty-five-cent package of Birds Eye frozen peas." According to him, "The consumer just couldn't understand how anything frozen could possibly be safe, let alone good to eat." One of the store owners, Joshua Davidson, who had taken over his father's business, was interviewed by *Quick Frozen Foods* magazine thirty years later and recalled, "I could see this as a sound venture, a progressive step in the food industry, and I wanted to be in step. That's why I agreed to be one of the first ten dealers." General Foods tried to make the venture as risk-free as possible. It supplied the freezer and the food, and the store owner had to pay General Foods only for what they sold. "Frankly," said Davidson, "I couldn't afford not to be, the way Birds Eye offered to start me."

Davidson said he was constantly answering questions about how the food was made and how to cook it. One woman asked whether the company would start packaging meat and vegetables together. Davidson dismissed the idea, pointing out that people would prefer to choose their menu themselves. It was twenty years before complete frozen dinners would become popular. Mostly people wanted to know whether the frozen food had any taste. Many people asked questions but would not buy. But after a month of answering questions, the amount of frozen food sold in Davidson's store doubled.

If you sell only one and then you sell two, you have doubled sales. In truth, frozen food was slow to catch on. One of the problems was that fresh food was relatively inexpensive. A top-quality steak often sold for less than 30 cents. It was inevitable that frozen food had to cost a few cents more than the fresh food it was made from, because of the labor and other costs that went into freezing it. The consumer was not accustomed to this idea, because in the past frozen food was made from the cheapest, rejected fresh food and so was cheaper than good fresh food. But to freeze top-quality fresh food with modern equipment was expensive.

The ad in the Springfield paper, which featured the new label—an upside-down bird and the name Birds Eye Frosted Foods—claimed the company's "frosted food" was "little short of magic." The haddock, it claimed, was "as fresh flavored as the day the fish was drawn from the cold blue waters of the North Atlantic." And "here is the most wondrous magic of all! June peas, as gloriously green as any you will see next summer. Red raspberries, plump and tender and deliciously flavored. Big, smiling pie cherries—and loganberries. Imagine having them all Summer-fresh in March!"

This kind of hyperbole continued for many years, not only by Birds Eye but by major newspapers and magazines. In February 1932 the *New York Times* called frozen food a "scientific miracle in home management." It reported on peaches, strawberries, and oysters becoming available out of season as though the frozen item and a fresh one were indistinguishable. *Popular Science Monthly* claimed outright that frozen food and fresh food were "exactly the same." Today's discerning palate knows that frozen and fresh are considerably different, but for people who were accustomed to canned food or slow-frozen food, the new frosted food did seem miraculous. Consumers who had the courage to try it were pleased with how much better it was than they had expected. When frozen fillets were test-marketed in New England, where people were accustomed to fresh fish, three out of four purchasers returned to buy more.

One of the major advantages of frozen food was that you could buy it immediately but use it whenever you wanted. The drawback, of course, was that few people had adequate home freezers to take advantage of the new phenomenon.

For the first decade of the Depression, food purchases went something like this: canned food was for the poor, and out-of-season frozen food was a high-quality luxury for the wealthy. It wasn't until the 1940s, when Birds Eye started getting competitors, that prices came down and frozen food became more widely popular. Finding a way to produce at an acceptable price was one of the keys to commercial success.

When Bob invented a portable multiplate freezer, a typical low-technology Birdseye invention, in 1930, it was built from scraps of corrugated metal, with steel plates and coils carrying refrigerant. It could be brought out to fields to freeze produce as it was harvested. This brought the farmer and the farm one step closer to industry, which for Bob and his generation was considered a very good move, since they thought of industry as an improvement. (Many of today's advocates of food quality think just the reverse.) Devices such as the portable freezer increased production capacity and even brought the price slightly lower on some vegetables—expensive vegetables in any form are difficult to sell.

By 1933 there were still only 516 retail stores in America carrying "frosted food." When the company questioned store owners, the chief complaint was about the store freezer units.

Though they were given to the stores, they used a great deal of electricity and were expensive to operate. Bob was not happy about the freezer either, as the Frosted Food Division was losing money and General Foods was growing impatient. Giving away a $1,500 freezer to any store that would have it was a losing proposition in a very bad economy.

From the beginning Bob had seen better freezers as a key to launching frozen food. He had wanted Wetmore Hodges as a partner in part because his father was with the American Radiator Company, which was interested in developing freezers. Bob wanted a more affordable and more attractive store freezer. He persuaded General Foods to back the development of a new American Radiator Company freezer that turned out to be a huge step forward for frozen food. It put the food on display, with a slanted window in the front; more important, a freezer cost just $300. This was a freezer that stores could afford. The monthly running cost was about $3.50, instead of the $16 to $20 of the old freezers. The new freezers were rented to stores for $10 to $12.50 per month. In 1934 they were tried out in Syracuse, New York. Stores bought them, and the frozen food sold well there. Another test was launched in Rochester; from there the refrigerators spread throughout the Northeast into the Midwest, well on their way to national distribution.

Bob used his own talent for persuasion, traveling to stores to sell his product in person. "He was one of the most articulate and persuasive men I have ever known," Joe Guinane said. Bob had also become a minor celebrity and was booked for events that advertised "see[ing] a demonstration of quick frosting by Mr. Clarence Birdseye, the inventor of the famous quick freezing process." Sometimes the public was also invited to "meet Mrs. Clarence Birdseye." Mostly women attended these demonstrations, but at one event in a Boston hotel Bob's old friend from Labrador Sir Wilfred Grenfell, the man who by chance introduced Bob to freezing, went to see the Birdseye demonstration.

While the Frosted Food Division was struggling to make a profit, there seemed no limit to the exaggerated praise that journalists, politicians, and businessmen were willing to bestow on the "Birdseye invention." In 1931 Boston mayor James Michael Curley hosted a dinner to honor Birdseye, calling him a genius "whose contribution to the welfare of mankind gives promise of being the greatest in volume and value in a half century of American history." After Birdseye gave a demonstration, freezing a steak with dry ice, the mayor stated that Birdseye's invention "will probably be a greater contributing factor in preventing wars in the future than battleships or any other agency because, after all, wars are caused by starvation."

As though he were still living in Labrador, struggling for fresh food, Bob ate whatever wildlife he found in Gloucester, including birds he trapped. He would freeze these catches to see if they froze well. He was particularly fond of coot, a variety of waterfowl. He also liked to investigate more abstract concepts of freezing. How long would frozen meat keep? Scientists believed there was no expiration date to frozen meat if it remained unexposed to air, though some speculated that frozen animal fat would deteriorate after a few centuries.

Bob reflected on the moose Eleanor shot in 1929, which was butchered and frozen, and portions of which would frequently be thawed out and served for dinner. A moose is a very large animal, but by 1933 there was nothing left except for the neck. Even Bob, who ate everything, did not like moose neck. It was tough and gamey. Would four years of freezing change it? He had to find out, so he thawed it and cooked it and, to his surprise, found it to be quite tender.

He hired a chemist experienced in food issues, Donald Tressler, to head the research team and arranged for Tressler and his family to move into his old home with the long shady porch on Beach Road. Birdseye and Tressler conducted experiments, measuring meat tenderness with a tire pressure gauge and a laboratory instrument called a penetrometer. They demonstrated that meat was more tender after a week of quick freezing than before it was frozen.

Bob still wanted to find out how the Inuit fish that had frozen in the air were alive months later when thawed. Could a living organism survive freezing? The question was more than a century old. When Bob would catch pickerel in nearby Niles Pond, he would try to freeze them and keep them alive. His oldest son, Kellogg, always remembered his patient mother's irritation at constantly finding fish flipping around in the bathtub or floating dead. Bob would explain to children in the neighborhood what he was trying to do, and it was generally assumed that it could not be done, that Mr. Birdseye was brilliant but a bit eccentric, though some thought that if Birdseye thought it was possible, it was.

Around that time, between 1934 and 1936, scientists in the Soviet Union were wondering about the same thing. They concluded that freezing did kill animals, but they noted the exception with fish. The scientists then demonstrated that when ice formed around the skin and the subcutaneous tissue directly under it, the fish would become hard and appear to be frozen, but the living organs inside would not freeze and could continue to function. In 1934 N. A. Borodin, in his study "The Anabiosis or Phenomenon of Resuscitation of Fishes after Being Frozen," concluded that it could be done and that Arctic species were particularly suited to survive freezing. The fish Birdseye had observed in Labrador were pulled into −40-degree air, and the water on them instantly froze, possibly leaving the interior of the fish unfrozen and unharmed.

Some of Bob's ideas seemed to be great successes even though they were never used, such as a machine he built to freeze vegetables individually rather than in a block. A pea would come down a chute and land on one of a series of revolving freezing plates. Though his laboratory was small and employed only twenty-two chemists and assistants, Bob was fondly remembered in Gloucester as someone who offered work through the Depression. In a 1980 article in the *Gloucester Daily Times*, Bill Nickerson, a former Birdseye worker, said, "There was nothing as far as jobs go then. Mr. Birdseye gave me a job right out of high school, when I couldn't find another one." He worked as a 30-cents-an-hour laboratory assistant.

In this laboratory the team worked out the problems of freezing vegetables, fruit, and prepared foods. They learned that vegetables degenerated due to an enzyme that could be removed by blanching them—plunging them quickly into boiling water. Then they were rapidly cooled, quick-frozen, and packed in watertight cellophane. This left the vegetables with a bright color. Frozen peas became one of the most successful Birds Eye foods, because they were such a brilliant green.

The laboratory also solved the problem of frozen sliced onions, which always turned black with freezing. They found that if the onions were first plunged into boiling water for just the right number of seconds, they would remain white. Fruits were difficult, because they softened and turned brown with freezing. The color change, caused by oxidation, was solved by adding a small amount of sulfur dioxide or ascorbic acid (vitamin C), but the lab was not able to completely solve the problem of texture. An expert from Cornell University, Lucy Kimball, was brought in to develop techniques for cooking prepared foods so that they would maintain their quality after being thawed and reheated.

Retailers complained that there was not a wide enough variety of products, so Bob established a partnership with a large farm in southern New Jersey, Seabrook Farms, to supply a greater variety of vegetables. While he tried to encourage farms to modernize and become more efficient, Seabrook was already an agro-industrial operation, supplying produce for canneries. In 1911 Charles Seabrook had started Seabrook Farms as a model of modern agro-industry. Birds Eye was able to have them wash, blanch, and cool produce for freezing in the new portable freezers. Lima beans, which had been a mainstay of Seabrook's cannery business, were one of their early frozen-vegetable successes.

However, certain foods were problem products and never conquered. Birdseye could not freeze lettuce without wilting it or tomatoes without ruining their texture, and frozen bananas were an utter disaster. But between 1932 and 1934 more than one hundred types of frozen foods, many of them processed, were developed. Most of them were not put on the market until the 1940s because of a lack of interest from the public. But Bob was always sure that the day would come for frozen food, and when it did, they needed to be ready. In the neighborhood around the Fort, one of Gloucester's poorest, which also included the broad, sandy Pavilion Beach, Bob would occasionally distribute samples of new products to children and ask for their opinions.

Tressler wrote of 1929, when the laboratory began its work, "This was the beginning of the depression but we did not realize it." By 1933 General Foods realized it. They still believed in the future of frozen food and continued to aggressively market it, but they had to cut their losses. They closed down Birdseye's Gloucester operation, worked out of Boston, and did not return to Gloucester until the 1940s.

Bob Birdseye went from president of the division to consultant. He continued to take an interest in the progress of frozen food and to promote it whenever he got a chance, sometimes without even being asked. But his restless mind moved on to other ideas.

CHAPTER NINE

The Crazy Guy Down the Street

Unaffected by the Depression, unlike most people, the Birdseyes had found the good life in their Eastern Point Wyndiecote. Bob enjoyed entertaining guests in his home and was extremely open and casual, while Eleanor was a little more formal and reserved. Bob loved to cook, and they had dinner parties in their large formal dining room with thrilling sea views. He specialized in what he liked to call "lobster feeds," in which he would triumphantly emerge from the kitchen sporting an apron and a chef's hat, carrying an enormous platter of steamed lobsters.

The Birdseyes owned five hundred acres of land in West Gloucester, a more rural area on the mainland (Gloucester was built on an island) where the wealthy retreated from the smell of drying fish in the hot summer months. There they built an elegant two-story riding stable with a long arcade. They kept fine Thoroughbred horses and rode with slim English saddles. Birdseye, who had lived on horseback in the

Southwest and in the Bitterroot, was an expert horseman, and he taught his children to ride.

Bob was still an outdoorsman and took his dogs duck hunting in South Dakota every year. He taught the whole family to shoot and sometimes took them with him on those trips. Based on the amount of film he shot of sunsets behind Gloucester harbor and whitecaps spraying over the dark crests of the granite boulders, Bob must have loved these views. He seemed to love Gloucester. He cooked seawater down to salt and carried that salt in a vial wherever he traveled. Despite the stiffness of his writing, Bob was a sentimental man.

He tried to take care of Eastern Point, preserving its bird habitat. He persuaded the government to build a seawall in a nearby cove to protect Niles Pond from storms. Behind his house he had chicken coops with long runs for Rhode Island Reds, the same species he and Eleanor had raised in Labrador. They also raised big, fluffy chinchillas. Bob remained relatively unchanged from his youth and continued to sell the pelts and freeze the meat.

His interest in the arts expanded, although he kept up past traditions. Buffalo Bill's Wild West was never a forgotten romance, and he was still an avid reader of Henty adventure novels, rereading his favorite, *Redskin and Cowboy*. He also read the western novels of Owen Wister, famous for his 1902 *The Virginian*, and the western stories of Bret Harte. He also enjoyed going to movies to see westerns or staying home to play Chinese checkers, a game for which he had a near-fanatical passion.

Bob was a curious figure in Gloucester, a famously inventive genius who did odd things that regular people would not understand. When rats invaded his melon patch, he stood on the terrace and shot them with a handgun. He was always trapping or shooting or freezing something as though he were surviving on the frontier. Children would ask him what he was doing, and he would always eagerly explain.

He often involved his family in his experiments and was eager for them to learn. Sometimes there was no particular purpose other than to satisfy his own curiosity, such as when he got an idea for a new way to make potato chips and enlisted the children in his kitchen experiments, along with his wife, Eleanor, when she did not run out of patience. His daughter Eleanor recalled a moment during her early childhood with her dad, learning how to dissect animals in the Persian-carpeted living room. He also taught her how to skin mice and cure skins.

When Josephine Swift Boyer was a child in California, her family spent summers at their home on Eastern Point. Like a number of girls in the neighborhood, she took up an interest in birds. When she found a dead rail, a wading bird rare for Gloucester, she wanted to keep it, and not knowing what to do with it, she went to curious Mr. Birdseye. Not surprisingly, he turned out to be a skilled taxidermist. He showed her how to open the bird up, rub it with chemicals, and stuff it. Josephine's sister, Lila, said that her clearest memory of him was of his fine hands. A reporter from the *New York Post*, interviewing him in 1945, wrote that he had "powerful hands," a surprising feature for such a small man.

"He was a character," Lila said. "You couldn't help being fascinated by him." This was true, as he was always building strange things in his large, high-ceilinged basement or in the kitchen or even on the lawn. Lila, who loved birds and even in her old age nursed wounded ones back to health, remembered a strange contraption on Mr. Birdseye's lawn. "It was for capturing starlings. We always thought he was going to eat them, probably fast frozen, taste-tested for some experiment. In any case, we knew they were goners."

The neighbors were further amused when, amid much discussion of food shortages during World War II, Bob reminded people that there was lots of food out there to shoot and eat and that "food tastes are principally psychological," as muskrats, crows, squirrels, and even *starlings* were delicious.

Bob was fascinated with processes and how to improve them. Writing about his curiosity, he explained:

> *If I see a man skinning a fish, for example, a host of questions pop into my mind. Why is he skinning the fish? Why is he doing it by hand? Is the skin good for anything? If I am in a restaurant and get biscuits, which I like, I ask the chef how he made them: what did he put in the dough? How did he mix it? How long did the biscuits bake? At what temperature? When I visit a strange city, I go through the local industrial plants to see how they make things. I don't care what the product is. I am just as much interested in the manufacture of chewing gum as of steel.*

While his kids were learning to be yachtsmen at the Eastern Point Yacht Club, he preferred to go fishing on his rugged, forty-foot, wooden-hulled, open-deck power launch, the *Sealoafer*. If he caught something interesting, he would do what he did with all the other animals he encountered: try freezing it. After trying to freeze whales and dolphins, he started to become interested in studying them. As was the family tradition, he had someone film him at sea. There was the small bald man with glasses, dressed in a sweater and dress shirt and tie, walking out on a narrow plank over the bow of his boat with an enormous harpoon, which, like Queequeg in *Moby-Dick*, he would raise up and hurl into the side of a six-foot shark or a porpoise or a whale.

Caught in 16-millimeter black and white is the same Bob Birdseye of the Bitterroot, a relentless predator. In one sequence he is harpooning porpoises (in the 1930s hunting marine mammals was still legal). He invented and patented the kickless, handheld whale harpoon to allow single-handed planting of the harpoon—much more efficient than throwing it himself, although Birdseye seemed effective enough with the old technique. Typical of Birdseye, it combines medieval technology with pragmatic inventiveness to solve a problem. The invention has an aluminum rifle stock and a thick tube of black rubber to propel the harpoons. The rubber is stretched back by the turning of a large steel cogwheel with a hand crank, and a trigger releases it to fire the harpoon. The tool was limited in its application and never caught on, but it served Bob well at sea for four years. According to him, he harpooned fifty-two finback whales, the second-largest animals to have ever lived on Earth.

Another time Bob got creative was when he watched commercial fishermen landing red snapper one winter in Galveston, Texas. The fishermen were hand lining, dropping a baited and weighted line many fathoms to the coral reefs on the ocean bottom. When they got a bite, they quickly reeled the line up on their circling two thumbs, the way hand liners have been fishing for centuries. Bob thought that there must be an easier way to do this, but when he talked to fishermen, they told him they had always fished this way and, since it worked, were not interested in changing.

This was absolutely contrary to the Birdseye creed. Bob always said, "Just because something has always been done in a certain way is never a sufficient reason for continuing to do it in that way." Birdseye believed in change, believed in the constant updating and improvement of ideas. He said, "Change is the very essence of American life" and frequently stated, "There is always a better way of doing almost everything. Today anything which is twenty years old is, or should be, apt to be obsolete."

Despite the protests of fishermen, Birdseye worked on the automatic reel: a device installed on the side of a boat that lowered a baited steel cable to depths greater than one hundred fathoms. When a fish bit, the reel set the hook and hauled it up to the surface. It could even land the fish on the deck. Birdseye felt he was onto the next big idea and boasted, "The gadget does everything, in fact, except mix a mint julep for the fisherman." He truly thought it would revolutionize commercial fishing, because in one day the device could catch as many fish as three fishermen. He predicted that it would "make more sea food available, and increase fishermen's earnings." Like many people in the 1930s, Birdseye was not thinking about the concept of overfishing, the idea that the survival of a fish population could be at risk if too many fish were caught. He never ended up developing the device. Had it become a tool of commercial fishing, it would have revolutionized the industry, but its destructive power would be unacceptable in today's overfished oceans, and it would likely be banned.

Bob's work with lightbulbs had greater success and far more impact. He noticed that reflectors were placed behind light-bulbs to illuminate displays in shopwindows. "I didn't know the difference between an ohm and a kilowatt," said Bob, "but it seemed to me there was no reason why the bulb and the reflector should be separate units. Wouldn't it be simpler and cheaper to build a lamp which would contain its own reflector?"

To answer his own question, he formed the Birdseye Electric Company, which provided even more jobs in Gloucester. His 1935 patent 2,219,510 for a reflecting electric lamp was one of his most important. Designed for working areas and window displays, his lightbulb with the built-in reflector is a component still in common use today. He designed more intensely glowing filaments for more efficient lighting and heat lamps for keeping food warm, another idea of his still used today. He also manufactured neon bulbs with a decorative figure inside that would light up, displaying flowers, animals, religious symbols, and occasional advertising logos, such as his RCA bulbs, all of which are rare and collectible today.

Birdseye developed ideas and used them to create a company, which he then would sell, as he had done with frozen food earlier. In 1939 Bob sold the Birdseye Electric Company to Wabash Appliance Corporation of Brooklyn, on the condition that Birdseye Electric would keep its own name and personnel. In 1945 the Sylvania Company bought Birdseye and Wabash out and continued producing Birdseye bulbs.

Despite the earlier troubles, Birdseye's frozen food became a popular commodity. In 1930 eighty thousand pounds of it were sold, and by the mid-1940s ten times that amount was being sold every year. Frozen food grew, as Birdseye had always said it would, from a mere curiosity to a major industry. Still, there were problems that did not involve consumers. For instance, the frozen-food industry was struggling to get enough well-insulated refrigerator trucks for shipping to their growing market. Birdseye and other advocates of frozen food were a major force in pushing Congress into its 1938 revision of the Pure Food and Drug Act. The 1906 act was considered a huge step forward in consumer safety, as it established rules for food and pharmaceuticals, including truth in labeling, but Bob felt that its standards were not nearly stringent enough for the frozen-food industry. Birds Eye had introduced high standards, and it was thought that the only way the industry could grow, as new companies were being created, was to make sure that all frozen food was held to those standards, so the public would start associating "frozen" with "quality."

Birds Eye now had competing frozen-food companies, and there was pressure to lower prices, but Bob always understood the risk of lowering quality to lower prices. Increased regulations were needed to stop producers from cutting corners on quality. The 1938 Food, Drug, and Cosmetic Act, which replaced the 1906 act, increased penalties, had a longer list of harmful commodities, had tougher rules about mislabeling and adulterating, and required a list of ingredients on every product's label. It remains the underpinning of product safety in the United States.

In the early 1940s, World War II changed the way Americans ate. A scarcity of metals led to a decline in canning, which led many people to try frozen food for the first time. But the biggest difference in Americans' eating habits was that women were allowed to leave their domestic roles to work wartime jobs while men were abroad. Many women would not return to the kitchen, or at least not full-time, so a trend of looking for quicker and easier ways to prepare meals began and has continued ever since. A 1951 survey in *Science Digest* found that 41 percent of US housewives preferred frozen food to either fresh or canned because of its convenience. In addition, there was a surge in the number of US supermarkets, which chose to give a great deal of their ample space to frozen foods. By 1950, according to the American Frozen Food Institute, 64 percent of US retail food stores carried some frozen food.

Despite the positive developments, it was not enough for Bob to be the guru of the last big food idea. He wanted to be master of the next. Birdseye was convinced that the next important food idea was dehydration, and he wondered whether a process that extracted the water from food more rapidly—quick-drying—would be the same kind of improvement as quick-freezing.

He began his work on dehydration in his kitchen, with a coffee hot plate hung upside down from the ceiling and a plate of bread cubes placed a few inches below. Then he brought in a favorite piece of Birdseye equipment, an electric fan, to blow on the bread. With both the heat and the air blowing, he stirred the bread with a spoon. Bob concluded that this process dehydrated faster than the standard technique of just blowing hot air. There were other techniques. Pouring milk on a heated stainless-steel drum dried it, and placing beef inside the heated drum produced dried beef for World War II soldiers. Yet all these techniques resulted in the loss of flavor and nutrients, so Bob analyzed the problem.

He knew there were three ways of transferring heat. Traditional dehydration relied solely on convection, the transfer of heat by moving warmed matter, which in this case was air. But there was also conduction, the movement of heat from atom to atom, thereby moving heat through the matter that is being warmed; and radiation, heating by means of heat waves, like those given off by the sun or, in Birdseye's case, by an infrared bulb he designed himself, drawing on his experience as a lamp manufacturer. Bob thought that the drying process could be greatly sped up and the quality better preserved if all three techniques were applied at once. It took him six years to find a way to substantially reduce the drying time, but when he accomplished it, he called the food he produced anhydrous, as opposed to dehydrated, just as his frozen food was called frosted. Food that had once taken eighteen hours to dehydrate took ninety minutes with Birdseye's process. He claimed that the food did not have time to deteriorate and could be restored to a fresh state in four to ten minutes. He gave demonstrations using his infrared lamp and at times held up a beaker of water he had extracted from an anhydrous carrot, a great crowd-pleasing trick, though that shortcut demonstration required that the carrot be previously heated and have air blown on it.

Understanding the age he lived in, Birdseye promised that his anhydrous food process would save the housewife time, because the food was already partially cooked. It would also save kitchen space, because a package the size of two cigarette packs would contain food for a family, and the small packets could be stored without the risk of spoilage, saving trips to the supermarket. He claimed tremendous savings for wholesalers when "five truckloads of farm produce can be processed into one truck load." The grocer, he promised, could save 80 percent of his shelf space.

With the outbreak of World War II, Bob thought his moment had come, because lightweight, portable, nonspoiling food seemed ideal for soldiers in the field. He therefore intensified his research, installing machinery in his basement, with trays of vegetables along the wall awaiting processing. By his own account, during the war he traveled thousands of miles to gather information and ideas about dehydration.

In November 1945, after World War II ended, Bob officially launched his anhydrous food line. The army had used a great deal of dehydrated soups, vegetables, and stews during the war, but the soldiers weren't happy about that. No one really liked the taste of dehydrated food, even if it was anhydrous—a word that no one understood. Bob was not deterred, as he had been ridiculed and doubted before, and now, since the name Birdseye was taken seriously in the food industry, the *New York Times* ran a story with the headline "A New Page Is Turned in the History of Food." Bob established another Gloucester business, called Process Incorporated, to produce his anhydrous foods, and a number of companies signed on to distribute them. He invited two hundred food experts to lunch at the Waldorf Astoria in New York, and not until the meal was over did he reveal that the broccoli, carrot, mashed potatoes, and apple tarts were all anhydrous. The diners were truly surprised.

Anhydrous food was granted a patent in May 1947, but it was not a huge success. Soon all the new companies dealing in anhydrous food had closed.

While Birdseye had predicted "unprecedented growth" for both frozen and dehydrated food after the war, he admitted that for dehydrated food to keep up with frozen, the products would have to be improved.

Americans bought 800 million pounds of frozen food in 1945 and 1946. The *New Yorker* ran an article on the future of frozen food that began:

> *Not since the appearance of the first glacier, a few eons ago, has there been any phenomenon to compare with the frigid giant that is now looming on the horizon of the American housewife in the shape of the frozen food industry.*

The article excitedly pointed out that there were now forty retail stores in Manhattan that sold nothing but frozen food and that twenty-two of them had opened in the past six months, with more of those retail stores "popping up" all over the United States. Freezer manufacturing was booming, and more and more people were buying freezers for their homes.

Once frozen orange juice came onto the market, in 1950, US annual frozen-food sales shot up to $1 billion and were projected to reach $50 billion by 1957. Frozen foods now came in an endless variety, although some were widely recognized as being inferior to fresh, like eggs, cheese, and certain fish, and other foods still could not be successfully frozen, such as cantaloupe, grapes, lettuce, and onions. Once the recipients of farms' castoff foods, frozen-food companies were now the customer of choice for many farmers, because they paid well, bought with regularity, and gave guidance on soil and other technical issues.

With the heightened demand for frozen food, other companies entered the marketplace, and Birds Eye had stiff competition. There were more than five hundred brands of frozen food. A leading competitor was William L. Maxson, a New Yorker who made frozen meals and sold them to the Naval Air Transport Service. The navy continued to use his frozen meals after the war, serving them on navy flights. By 1950 Maxson had competition of his own: Frigid Dinners, Inc., of Philadelphia. But like Birdseye, Maxson saw an opportunity and the need for new technology, leading to his invention called the Maxson Whirlwind, an oven that thawed and cooked meals quickly.

Maxson's new oven was the beginning of a new age. It started with an accidental discovery in 1945, when an engineer at Raytheon, working on radar, found that his equipment produced unusually short radio waves, or microwaves, that rotated molecules and produced heat. This type of heat could be easily produced and, among other potential uses, could cook food rapidly. Bell Laboratories had done work on the idea in the 1930s. Now, with frozen food becoming commonplace, it was understood that microwaves could thaw a package of frozen food and cook it quickly. Frozen food could now be cooked and on the dinner table mere minutes after it had been removed from the freezer. This was the fastest food ever seen.

In another harbinger of the future, after the war the United States became interested in importing frozen seafood on a large scale from its new friend, Japan. Small amounts had been imported before the war from both Japan and India. Today frozen Asian seafood is a major component of the US fish market.

To deal with the increased competition, Birds Eye advertised innovatively and aggressively. It was one of the first to advertise in color in *Life* magazine, in 1940, and went on to become a pioneer television advertiser in the 1950s. It even sponsored its own situation comedy, *Our Miss Brooks*, in which Eve Arden played a schoolteacher—one of the first TV hits when it was launched in 1952.

Bob always believed in the central concept of agro-industry, through which technology would one day eliminate hunger in the world. He followed new industrial food ideas with great excitement. He was well aware of progress in microwaves and often mentioned it as one of the ideas of the future. He also believed in hydroponic farming, by which plants are provided nutrients in the water they are given, cutting out the need for soil and fields to grow crops. Hydroponic farming was not a new idea—Sir Francis Bacon wrote about it in the seventeenth century. But Bob envisioned a New York City whose produce needs were locally met, thanks to rooftop hydroponic farming. He predicted that "eventually we shall learn to manufacture food from sunlight, as plants do." And he also believed in the increasing use of antibiotics in food to prevent its decay, a practice that became widespread and is today often criticized as unhealthy.

CHAPTER TEN

The Last Idea

Often, when adventurous people start glimpsing old age and death, they are consumed with the urge to stave off time with one last adventure.

Bob and Eleanor were such people. Perhaps they recalled the words of Bob's old friend Wilfred Grenfell, who more than thirty years before had advised, "If you are reasonably resistant, and want to get tough and young again, you can do far worse than come and winter on 'the lonely Labrador.'"

Grenfell's words rang true for Bob and Eleanor. They wanted to go on an adventure, as they had when they went to Labrador. They wanted to leave their house and garden and push off one last time, especially since their children were grown and on their own.

Bob and Eleanor had always been sentimental about Labrador, perhaps in the way other couples are nostalgic about their first years of marriage, and they frequently spoke of their time up north. Throughout the years in Gloucester, with lobster dinners, evenings of home movies, and games of Chinese checkers, a pair of Labrador snowshoes always hung on a wall of their home.

The opportunity to go abroad showed up unexpectedly, like an intriguing uninvited guest. Still interested in food processing, Bob was visiting a lard-rendering plant in the 1940s, and something about the process started him thinking about a better way of converting wood chips into paper pulp. He did what he had always done: brought together some financial backers and some technical people and invented something new—in this case, a process for making paper.

Throughout history, many materials, including stone, clay, bamboo, Egyptian papyrus reeds, and dried animal skins were used for writing. But the most practical material was paper, invented by the Chinese possibly as long ago as 200 BC. Paper is made from the random weaving of fibers suspended in water. For many centuries the leading source of these fibers was old rags. Many other fibers were tried, including grasses, rhubarb, straw, and even animal excrement. In the mid-nineteenth century, ground wood pulp was settled on as the cheapest and most efficient source of paper fibers.

Perhaps because of the success with wood pulp, there was not a great deal of interest in Bob's ideas. But there were always a few papermakers interested in alternatives to grinding up trees. The New York–based W. R. Grace & Co. was one of a number of companies in the mid-twentieth century interested in using sugarcane for paper, and they were drawn to the Birdseye paper process.

Grace was a large old international company founded by an Irish immigrant in Peru, William Russell Grace. He became involved in the export of guano (bird droppings). This material may not seem like much, but it is rich in nitrogen and phosphorous, making it valuable in the manufacture of gunpowder and fertilizer. Even today guano remains a prospering South American trade. A steamship company called the Grace Line was created to ship the product, and that itself became a success. Thanks to shipments of guano, sugar, and fertilizer, by the 1950s W. R. Grace had operations in New York, London, Peru, Chile, and other places and owned the Grace National Bank, the Grace Chemical Company, and other businesses around the world.

Grace hoped to apply Birdseye's process to the production of paper from sugarcane scrap in Peru. A number of countries were suffering from acute paper shortages and had more cane than wood pulp. Peru was one of them. Grace found other potential markets for the paper process in Puerto Rico, Venezuela, Argentina, and Egypt.

Since Grace's Peruvian sugar fields produced a half million tons of sugar annually, as well as molasses and industrial-grade alcohol, mountains of crushed cane stalks and bagasse, or leftover crushed cane, were left behind. Bagasse was a fibrous substance perfectly suited to papermaking, and Grace already made paper with it, but his process was slow and inefficient, since it took six months to dry the bagasse enough to render it useful. With Birdseye's process, the useful cellulose fibers could be separated quickly from bagasse, and it might be possible to use the bagasse immediately. Grace thought Birdseye could greatly improve the company's paper process and built a large-output factory for it that would be a model to sell to other countries.

Bob loved the challenge, and he loved the idea of taking off for "the wilds" of South America. In 1953 he and Eleanor left their Wyndiecote by the sea in Gloucester and moved to Paramonga, the mountainous, cactus-studded desert of southern Peru. He quickly proved he was the same old Bob Birdseye, always thinking of adventure or food and writing home to report on it all to the family.

Bob was cooking, he was shooting birds with the shotgun he managed to bring in from the United States, and he started riding horses again, something he hadn't done since 1934 in West Gloucester. The terrain in Peru reminded him of the American Southwest, where he'd ridden almost a half century earlier. He also was doing a lot of fishing, and one day, while fishing in about forty feet of water, he felt a powerful tug on his line. He fought for thirty minutes to bring up what he thought would be an enormous fish, but it turned out to be a penguin. Once on the boat, the penguin continued to fight until they tied its feet and rubber-banded its sharp beak. Billy the penguin became a household pet.

Billy was not the only pet. The Birdseyes later adopted a deer and a redheaded parrot they named Pancho, which couldn't fly because Bob had accidentally clipped its wing while hunting. The Birdseyes resumed their old habit of raising Rhode Island Reds for their egg supply, and there were geese, ducks, squab, and guinea pigs around the house, though most of them ended up being eaten. The Birdseyes had a fifteen-cubic-foot General Electric freezer to keep a supply of meat for entertaining. Appropriately, they had the first freezer ever used in Paramonga, where most people didn't have refrigerators yet.

In the spring of 1954 Bob and Eleanor went back to the United States for almost two months, as Bob had patents to register. He and Eleanor also had the Gloucester home to check in on, children and grandchildren to see, and Henry and Ernestine's wedding in Albuquerque to attend. It was like one of those trips home from Labrador: a little business, a little shopping, and family gatherings. While in New York, Bob even phoned contacts at the American Museum of Natural History whom he hadn't used since 1910 and arranged for them to ship him taxidermy equipment and materials so he could send them bird specimens, similar to what he'd done in Labrador. When he returned to Paramonga, he killed four types of doves and several other birds and froze them until the package arrived from the museum. Over the next six months he killed and preserved specimens of sixty bird species and preserved forty mammal hides.

His inherent enthusiasm continued to drive him, even though at age sixty-eight he looked thin and uncharacteristically frail. During his two years in Peru he had learned how to reduce what had been a nine-hour papermaking process to only twelve minutes. Now he was eager to market it around the world, so in 1955 the Birdseyes left Paramonga again, abandoning Susie the fox, Billy the penguin, and Pancho the parrot. They might have preferred to go home to Gloucester, but Bob had work in New York City with the Grace company, so they rented an ample, well-furnished apartment at the Gramercy Park Hotel, opposite the leafy park.

From New York he assured *Time* magazine that "still

other ventures are afoot, and the days are not long enough for me to take advantage of all the opportunities I see." Doctors advised him to slow down, but he always insisted that "enthusiasm and hard work are also indispensable ingredients of achievement."

On October 9, 1956, at the age of sixty-nine, Clarence Birdseye died in his apartment in the Gramercy Park Hotel. He had asked that, rather than sending flowers to his funeral, people contribute to an Amherst College scholarship fund. He'd never forgotten how it felt to abandon his college education because of a lack of money. He didn't want other young men and women to go through that hardship. He asked to be cremated and have his ashes scattered in the sea off Gloucester, the place he so loved.

When Bob Birdseye passed away in 1956, frozen food had already become a multibillion-dollar international industry. It had been developing in Great Britain since the end of World War II, and eleven years after Bob Birdseye's death he became a fictitious British character called Captain Birdseye, a respectable, white-bearded old salt in a naval uniform who promoted frozen food. Few British people knew that there was a real Clarence Birdseye who had started the industry. The year Bob died, Giovanni Buitoni started the Italian frozen-food industry with frozen lasagna and ravioli. The ice cream industry was completely revolutionized by Bob's ideas on creating an entire frozen-food infrastructure, from factories to warehouses to trucks to stores.

Today frozen food is a major international business very similar to what Birdseye in the 1920s imagined it would become. Frozen Asian seafood exports alone account for billions of dollars in sales. Every country that has a food-export business exports frozen-food products. Many of Birdseye's ideas about industrialized food are not universally beloved today, but in many ways he would find this a world he had not only imagined but helped build. It is, as he predicted, a world in which food transcends geography and climate—any food, anywhere, at any time of year. Frozen food is an essential part of modern living—what modern home is complete without a freezer?

Birdseye's improbable ideas about frozen food changed our world, and that is what he is most remembered for.

Perhaps the more important thing about Clarence Birdseye was his ability to live life as an adventure. Curiosity is the one essential ingredient to an adventurous life.

acknowledgments

A warm thanks to all of my friends in Gloucester, and a special thanks to the Birdseye family for their kindness, generosity, and openness—Michael, Kelly, Gypsy, and Henry, thank you so very much. And great thanks to the American Museum of Natural History for science advice. Thanks to my agent, Charlotte Sheedy, and to my patient and wise editor, Beverly Horowitz, for guiding this book through publication.

CREDITS

Frontispiece: Courtesy of the Birdseye family. Birds Eye® is a registered trademark of Pinnacle Foods Group LLC.

INSERT
Page 1
Top: Courtesy of Rocky Mountain Laboratories, NIAID.
Middle: Amherst College Archives and Special Collections, Clarence Birdseye (AC 1910) Journals [vol. 3], pp. 42–43. Used with permission of the Birdseye family.
Bottom: Courtesy of the Birdseye family.

Page 2
Top: The Rooms Provincial Archive Division, VA 16–21. *The Bungalow, Muddy Bay*/Rev. Henry C. Gordon, [1921–1922], Henry Cartwright Gordon fonds.
Bottom: Courtesy of the Birdseye family.

Page 3
Top: Courtesy of the Birdseye family.
Bottom: World-Telegram Photo/C.M. Stieglitz. The *New York World-Telegram* and the *Sun Newspaper* Photograph Collection (Library of Congress).

Page 4
From the *Springfield Sunday Union and Republican*, March 2, 1930; p. 20 A. Birds Eye® is a registered trademark of Pinnacle Foods Group LLC.

Page 5
Top: Courtesy of the Birdseye family.
Bottom: Courtesy of the Birdseye family. Birds Eye® is a
registered trademark of Pinnacle Foods Group LLC.

Page 6
Top: Cape Ann Museum, Gloucester, MA, USA.
Bottom: Cape Ann Museum, Gloucester, MA, USA. Birds Eye®
is a registered trademark of Pinnacle Foods Group LLC.

Page 7
Top: Courtesy of the Birdseye family.
Bottom: Courtesy of the Birdseye family.

Page 8
Top left: Courtesy of the Birdseye family.
Top right: Courtesy of the Birdseye family.
Bottom: Cape Ann Museum, Gloucester, MA, USA.

BIBLIOGRAPHY

BOOKS

Carlton, Harry. *The Frozen Food Industry*. Knoxville: University of Tennessee Press, 1941.

Dolin, Eric Jay. *Fur, Fortune, and Empire: The Epic History of the Fur Trade in America*. New York: W. W. Norton, 2010.

Evans, Harold. *They Made America: From the Steam Engine to the Search Engine: Two Centuries of Innovators*. With Gail Buckland and David Lefer. New York: Little, Brown, 2004.

Foley, John. *The Food Makers: A History of General Foods Ltd.* Banbury, Oxfordshire: General Foods, 1972.

Freidberg, Susanne. *Fresh: A Perishable History*. Cambridge, Mass.: Belknap Press of Harvard University Press, 2009.

Fucini, Joseph, and Suzy Fucini. *Entrepreneurs: The Men and Women Behind Famous Brand Names and How They Made It*. Boston: G. K. Hall, 1985.

Grenfell, Wilfred Thomason. *Adrift on an Ice-Pan*. Boston: Houghton Mifflin, 1909.

_____. *A Labrador Doctor: The Autobiography of Wilfred Thomason Grenfell*. Boston: Houghton Mifflin, 1919.

_____. *Tales of the Labrador*. Boston: Houghton Mifflin, 1916.

Tressler, Donald, and Norman W. Desrosier, eds. *Fundamentals of Food Freezing*. Westport, Conn.: Avi, 1977.

Tressler, Donald, and Clifford F. Evers. *The Freezing and Preservation of Foods.* 2 vols. Westport, Conn.: Avi, 1957.

U.S. Patent Office. *Selected Patents of Clarence Birdseye.*

Williams, E. W. *Frozen Foods: Biography of an Industry.* Boston: Cahner's, 1968.

NEWSPAPER, MAGAZINE, AND JOURNAL ARTICLES

Birdseye, Clarence. "Looking Backward at Frozen Foods." *Refrigerating Engineering,* November 1953.

_____. "Postwar Problems of the Frozen Food Industry." *Meals for Millions.* Final Report of the New York State Joint Legislative Committee on Nutrition, 1947.

Burton, L. V. "Birdseye Demonstrates New Twenty-Plate Froster." *Food Industries,* November 1941.

Farrell, Morgan. "Quick Food Freezing Process Devised to Aid the Housewife." *New York Times,* February 14, 1932.

Harris, Herbert. "The Amazing Frozen-Foods Industry." *Science Digest,* February 1951.

Kahn, F. J., Jr. "The Coming of the Big Freeze." *The New Yorker,* September 14, 1946.

Kenyon, Paul. "About the Birdseyes . . . and More." *Gloucester Daily Times,* April 14, 1978.

CHRONOLOGY OF UNSIGNED ARTICLES

"For the First Time Anywhere! The Most Revolutionary Idea in the History of Food Will Be Revealed in Springfield Today." *Springfield Union,* March 6, 1930.

"Mayor Praises Clarence Birdseye for Work in Refrigeration Field." *Boston Globe,* July 8, 1931.

"Continuous Quick Freezer Developed by Birdseye." *Food Industries,* September 1940.

"Dinner, Frozen or Dried." *Newsweek,* November 19, 1945.

"Meet Mr. Birdseye—He Had a $22,000,000 Idea." *Look*, April 30, 1946.

"Birdseye Changes Pace, Now Raises Wildflowers." *Cape Ann Summer Sun*, August 17, 1950.

"Father of Frozen Foods Dies: Clarence Birdseye Dead at 69." *Gloucester Daily Times*, October 8, 1956, 1.

"Clarence Birdseye Is Dead at 69; Inventor of Frozen Food Process." *New York Times*, October 9, 1956.

WEBSITES

The Internet is full of inaccurate information on Birdseye, most of it feeding off each other. But there are a few useful sites:

amherst.edu (for information about the Birdseyes at Amherst)
foodreference.com (for a food time line)
library.hbs.edu (for a list of deals involving General Foods)

Index

ABOUT THE AUTHOR

MARK KURLANSKY is the *New York Times* bestselling author of *Ready for a Brand New Beat: How "Dancing in the Street" Became the Anthem for a Changing America; The Food of a Younger Land; Cod: A Biography of the Fish That Changed the World; Salt: A World History; 1968: The Year That Rocked the World;* and *The Big Oyster: History on the Half Shell,* among other books. He lives in New York City.